MY GRANDFATHER

My Grandfather

DENIS CONSTANDUROS

BBC BOOKS

B orn in 1910, Denis Constanduros escaped a formal education and had, instead, a succession of private tutors. He was only 15 when he sold his first cartoon caricatures, of Wimbledon players and characters, to the press. Later, he went to Chelsea Art School and produced Shell posters at the same time as Graham Sutherland and McKnight Kauffer.

At the age of 27 he had his first radio play produced, although he had already collaborated with his aunt, Mabel Constanduros, on some of the *Buggins Family* sketches.

The mother of Denis Constanduros was a daughter of Richard Tilling of the successful Tilling Transport group. The two daughters married two brothers of the Constanduros family. Denis's father was an unqualified architect and a compulsive gambler, and his mother and father parted company after the First World War.

In 1938, Denis Constanduros married Barbara Neill and moved to Wiltshire. Classified unfit, although he had at one time been mixed doubles champion of Portugal, he spent much of the Second World War working in the office of a munitions factory. In 1948, he had his first television play accepted and *My Grandfather* was published.

The West Country radio serial Denis Constanduros created and wrote, *At the Luscombes*, ran for 16 years. He adapted many classic novels for television during the 1960s and 1970s, including works by H. G. Wells, Henry James and Jane Austen, and died in 1978.

Published by BBC Books
a division of BBC Enterprises Ltd
Woodlands, 80 Wood Lane, London W12 0TT

First published 1948 by Longmans, Green and Co. Ltd

This edition published 1989

© *The author 1948*

ISBN 0 563 20864 3

PRINTED AND BOUND IN GREAT BRITAIN BY RICHARD CLAY, BUNGAY, SUFFOLK
COVER PRINTED BY RICHARD CLAY, NORWICH

PREFACE

IN the early days, when my grandfather lived in his big, gloomy house on Sydenham Hill, it was my secret delight to slip away up the back stairs to the boxroom and poke about among the discarded dolls' prams and broken rocking horses, to lift dust sheets from antiquated furniture or broken crockery, in the hope of finding something—but what I do not know. Everything in the boxroom seemed to have a peculiar lustre and attraction. (I remember particularly well a picture of 'The Charge of the Light Brigade' with Tennyson's poem underneath. It was the *pièce de résistance* of the whole exciting show.) Every object seemed to have a new and a deeper significance for having been thrown away and re-discovered in private. Each bulging dust sheet was pregnant with unlimited possibilities and there was a fine excitement about lifting a corner and finding, perhaps, a child's cooking stove, a pair of old riding boots, some bound magazines and a broken commode, all jumbled together in splendid confusion.

There is a very obvious resemblance between one's mind, in later years, and my grandfather's boxroom; for sights and sensations, opinions and experiences are stored away with the same haphazard abandon. As time goes by the accumulation of personal rubbish proceeds until the mental bric-à-brac of years fills the mind to overflowing with a rich and varied store of junk which can yield unlimited wealth to the careful scavenger. And there is the same excitement in lifting a corner of the memory, to find an inconsequent heap of treasures, each covered with the fictitious patina of all that has remained long under the dust sheet. Even the useless or the downright ugly seemed alluring in my grandfather's boxroom; so it is with one's memory. Look at the number of people who swear that their school days were the happiest in their lives. I don't believe a word of it; but I do believe that if it were possible to return from hell we should hear, not about the tortures of purgatory, but of happy days in the fiery furnace and of the sing-songs and good times enjoyed by the damned souls—all told with a veneer of nostalgic sentimentality. It is almost impossible to remember unpleasant things, at least with the surface of the mind, for the mind digests and transmutes all that it assimilates, like the stomach, and, again like it, all that is too disagreeable it generally ejects.

People and scenes recollected over a long period of time, then, are apt to have a false lustre and, seen in long perspective, one's childhood frequently has the gem-like brightness of something seen through the wrong end of opera glasses. So I make no claim that these memories of my grandfather are in any way accurate. I merely state that they are as I found them: the junk in my own personal boxroom.

CONTENTS

CHAPTER ONE

MY GRANDFATHER AT THE WINDOW

EVERY summer evening, at the same time, an unusual sound would detach itself from the general buzz and hubbub of traffic down Kensington Gore. It was a sound from the past, a sound of carriage wheels and horses' hoofs, a rumbling, clattering, jangling sort of a noise that contrasted strangely with the smooth, impersonal hum of taxis, buses and private cars of the late nineteen-twenties as they sped, all too efficiently, to their unpredictable destinations. As soon as he heard it my grandfather would jump to his feet from the arm-chair where he had been enjoying the first cigar of the day and hurry on his short, stumpy legs to the window in time to see a coach, with brasses glittering and paint newly gleaming, clatter by in the afternoon sunlight.

It was a fine sight against the plane trees of Kensington Gardens; all the finer, it seemed, for being slightly absurd—consciously absurd, but nevertheless dignified, like a ship in full sail amid dirty, utilitarian tramp steamers. It was, I believe, the last coach to run a regular service and was maintained merely at the whim of some enthusiast. It seems almost too perfect a coincidence that its route should have been right past my grandfather's front door and, consequently, his study window, for nothing could have been more appropriate or have given him greater pleasure than this sight. Nor, in their turn, could the horses, the driver and the guard have had a more critical or more appreciative audience than my grandfather, as he stood at the old-fashioned casement window which, owing to the gradual sagging of the frame, was so difficult to open, and puffed with fat contentment at his first cigar.

In appearance he was short and round, with a face that was cherubic in its benignity. With his round, red face, his silver hair and, above all, his air of happy simplicity, he seemed a compound of Mr. Jorrocks, whom he read, admired and quoted, My Uncle Toby —though he had not read *Tristram Shandy* and would not, I suspect, have liked it in any case—and, most striking resemblance of all, his great hero, Mr. Pickwick.

As he stood at the window with the cigar in his hand, chumping his false teeth slightly and, perhaps, whistling under his breath "O Rest in the Lord" or a favourite air from "The Beggar's Opera", the likeness was remarkable. Could it have been a life-long devotion to Dickens, and Pickwick in particular, that brought it about? From early photographs he seems to have been a grave, almost sickly young man, deeply preoccupied with the labours of founding a business and providing for an ever-increasing family. (Then, in middle years, there is a photograph of him in full hunting clothes standing beside his horse in a little walled garden. What problems this poses! How did the horse get in there? Did my grandfather, with a fabulous leap, clear the high brick wall with its fruit trees, or did he come clattering through the drawing-room and out of the french windows?) It is not until later, when wealth and position are assured, that one can see the beginnings of the metamorphosis. At first there are added the spectacles,

13

then his whole body seems to sink and expand and there comes about him that glowing aura of genial content which is the true essence of Pickwickianism. Even his clothes were cut in a bygone fashion, for he still wore, in 1928, trousers with no turn-ups which fitted closely to the thigh and should have been strapped under the instep. Indeed, though he was the mildest and most gentle of men, he had a few most violent prejudices. One was against red-haired men, who he said were untrustworthy, and one was against boots with toe-caps. "You might as well", he used to say, "wear a feather in your hat as toe-caps on your boots."

As the coach, then, passed the Albert Hall with its broad pavements and its hoardings which announced such various attractions as Symphony Concerts, Oratorios, performances of "Hiawatha" and Boxing Tournaments, the scarlet-coated guard would rise to his feet and, drawing the coaching horn from its long wicker container, would blow in honour of my grandfather such a fine, resounding, exhilarating, ridiculous fanfare: a triumphant call from the warm, stable-smelling, gas-lit past of London, that it brought my grandmother and her sisters—'The Aunts'—to the long drawing-room window above, where they had been banished to prevent them irritating my grandfather after his day at the office. Aunt Maria

14

would pause for a moment in her game of Patience, for the sound, connected in her mind with my grandfather who, with King Edward the Seventh, was the only man in whom she had shown any interest, would penetrate her self-insulated brain. "Is that the coach, Sophy?" she would ask my grandmother. An hour before she had asked: "Is Richard in yet, Sophy?" and, content to know that he was safely home, she would continue with her Patience without further sign of animation.

But Aunt Pem, who was a few years younger, would run to the window at the first sound of the coach, laughing immoderately until the veins on the side of her fragile head stood out in blue relief. She laughed immoderately, not because she was particularly amused, but because it was the only way in which she could show emotion. Unlike most of her contemporaries she did not turn easily to tears, but turned instead to perpetual, uncontrollable giggles.

The sight of horses made her laugh more than anything, for she loved horses above all else. "Look, Maria, you lazy old girl", she would say from the window, laughing until the tears ran down her cheeks at this fine, unforgettable sight. But Aunt Maria would sit on at her Patience, a stolid, black, unlovely figure in the soft afternoon sunlight that slanted through the glass roof of the little conservatory at the end of the drawing-room. To her it was just another coach. She had seen many coaches pass innumerable windows and they all looked much the same. She might, perhaps, make some cryptic remark about how long the run took and what time it reached certain points on its route, for she had a remarkable knowledge of uninteresting statistics and a habit of making the most bald, ungarnished statements of unimportant facts during meal times that reminded my grandfather of Mr. F.'s aunt, and he would quote with deep pleasure: " 'There's milestones on the Dover Road'," or " 'When we lived at somewhere (I forget where), somebody's (I forget whose) geese was stole by tinkers.' " He delighted to quote from his beloved Dickens, and my mind is full of these fragmentary, inaccurate and half-erased quotations that remind me, not of Dickens, but of my grandfather, puncturing the end of his cigar, the silver cigar cutter held awkwardly in his short, paw-like hands, his amiable face glowing with the satisfaction of an apt quotation from his favourite author.

It was a moment of pride for my grandmother too, when the coach passed, for she was the only one of her family who was married, and this fine blast on the horn as it passed the house was a tribute, through my grandfather, to her, and thus accentuated her position of authority among the sisters.

Several times a year the Aunts were bidden from the obscurity of Croydon to stay at Kensington Gore and, though it would be unfair to say that my grandmother was patronizing, she was unable to resist the temptation to exploit small triumphs over her unmarried sisters. Thus, though it was not wartime, she forbade Aunt Maria to have more than one lump of sugar in her tea, with the result that Aunt Maria stole a supply and kept it in her handbag. Once, when drawing her handkerchief out of her bag—which she did all too seldom—she drew out with it several lumps of illicit sugar which clattered loudly all over the polished drawing-room floor in the middle of Sunday afternoon tea.

The sound of the coach, then, with its moment of triumph for my grandfather, brandishing his cigar and beaming all over his round, red face in answer to the most gracious bow, the condescending tilt of a silk hat from the driver and the passenger on the box next to him, was a moment of reflected glory upstairs in the long drawing-room with its two old ladies at the windows overlooking the Gardens and its third figure, stiff, black and incongruous in the glass-filtered sunlight of the conservatory at the farther end.

It was a moment of triumph on the next floor, too, where old Lucy, pale, thin and perpetually worried, in spite of forty years of complete security in my grandfather's household, was turning down the beds, muttering uneasily to herself, frowning at the possibility of some imagined disaster and dabbing the sheets to her puckered face to make doubly sure that they were aired. To Lucy tragedy was lurking everywhere, in every speck of germ-laden dirt, in each unaired garment or scrap of carelessly prepared food. Life for her was one long battle with the forces of darkness in an acutely domestic form.

"Tell yer Papa to mind the 'usks," she would say, her face flushed and distraught with anxiety as she handed a plate of porridge round the dining-room screen. In her mind she was handing him his death warrant and she could foresee with awful certainty the scene in which he would drop, choking and apoplectic, to the ground, killed by the carelessness of some scatterbrained kitchen-maid. It was Lucy who decided that a purple bath mat was too bright for my grandfather and, rising suddenly from his daily cold bath, the sight of it might cause him a stroke.

Up two more flights of stairs old Ellen, resting on her bed before preparing the dinner, also heard the horn. It meant little to her. She need not go down for another half hour—"Cook, damn you!" she would say to the chicken as she pushed it viciously into the oven—and the 'young girl' could make the bread sauce and put on the vegetables. She was the exact reverse of her life-long friend, Lucy. Where one was thin the other was correspondingly fat; where one was perpetually shadowed by impending doom the other was jolly, carefree and unmindful of the future. "Eat as much as you like," she used to say to the children in earlier days, on the rare occasions when she was left to look after them. "Here, take the sugar basin and get on with it, only for heaven's sake don't make yourself sick." While poor Lucy would hover round, her face charged with foreboding, saying: "Oh no, Ellen! Oh well, there—I don't know. No, Winnie dear, not any more sugar, dear. Tst, tst! Well there—I don't know, I'm sure." And she would stumble out of the room on her gnarled feet unable to bear the spectacle of her beloved children rushing headlong to destruction.

In a few brief seconds the moment had passed and the coach, clattering across the top of Queen's Gate, would diminish until it had become nothing but a faint, rhythmic beat of hoofs again, to be swallowed and absorbed in the utilitarian spate of hooting, grinding taxis, private cars and buses. Kensington Gore and the Gardens opposite, which slipped so easily into the past again, would take some moments to readjust themselves to a less picturesque present, and the ordinary every-day traffic, for some time after the coach had gone, rumbling and glittering, into the distance, would look like some grim vision of the future.

In the drawing-room my grandmother would turn away from the window to continue writing her letters, while Aunt Pem stood watching the coach out of sight as it followed the curve of the road round to-wards Kensington Palace, with the smile still left, forgotten, on her face. Lucy, as the hoofbeats died away, would dab the sheet to her cheek once more and mutter: "Well there, 'tis be 'opes 'e won't catch 'is death." Upstairs in the bedroom under the roof, with the two framed oleographs of unbelievably blue-eyed little girls with pink sashes, one called "My Mother Bids Me Bind My Hair" and the companion "When Lubin Is Away", which Lucy had rescued from the dismantled nursery because, as she said, they were so "sweet pretty", old Ellen would yawn and set her mind at rest for another half hour.

Glowing from the warmth of that fanfare in his honour and the condescension of those deferentially tilted silk hats, like a stone that still reflects the mid-day heat after sundown, my grandfather would turn back into the study, clicking his false teeth and hum-ming to himself "O Rest in the Lord". Then smiling, as it always seemed, from head to foot—no great distance for him—he would stump across to the farthest, darkest recess of the study, where a tray was always placed in the most inaccessible spot, at his own request, so that he might not too easily resort to it and so that, when he did, he might feel the drink well earned, and pour himself out a first, but generous, whiskey and soda.

CHAPTER TWO

SUNDAY AFTERNOON

Beside my grandfather's arm-chair there was a small smoker's table with, on the top, a scene, carved in soft wood, of a log cabin inhabited by bears. Half way up, just under the eaves, the cabin was hinged and the roof, folding back, allowed one to keep pipes or tobacco inside. There were several ash trays screwed to the table outside the cabin which, owing to a surprising lack of invention on the part of the carver, were intended to look like nothing but what they were, and among these wooden bears perpetually played, while one bear, most memorable of all, stood poking his head out of the cabin door which, like a stable door, opened at the top.

The whole piece of furniture, so large for such a comparatively small use, was in a heavily Swiss-Victorian style, but to a child, as I first remember it, standing in the draped and beeswaxed billiard room of my grandfather's previous house—a vast, Edwardian building in the forgotten backwater of Sydenham Hill—it was entrancing. The only disappointment was that, when one opened the lid to see more of the jovial bear which leaned out of the cabin door, one disclosed a contemptible deceit for, below the level of the door, where he was invisible from the outside, the bear was uncarved and merely degenerated into a block of meaningless wood. Nevertheless it was, in my mind, as indispensable an accessory to my grandfather as the white moustache or the slip-on glasses that he used for reading and which he would frequently leave upstairs in another pocket, sending one of his grandsons to fetch them with a genial: "Thank you, my boy—when you're my age I'll do the same for you."

It is through this table and some other relics of the past that I can best visualize my grandfather and his household in the years before I knew him. It breathes again, through its smell of pine wood and tobacco, the essence of an era which, seen in retrospect, seems like one long Sunday afternoon. There the table stood, unused, in the billiard room, with its seats at the end raised on curved platforms, with horsehair peeling from the upholstery, on which no one ever sat. There it remained, unused and forgotten, through that long, long Sunday afternoon, while discreetly silent servants, soft footed and whispering, flicked it with feather dusters and while the pipes of the central heating gurgled and burbled in their dutiful efforts to heat the billiard players who never came.

In summer the sunlight would stream through Venetian blinds turned down, like demure eyelids, to prevent the fading of materials or the bleaching of wood, while outside, in the wide deserted streets, a barrel organ would be tinkling gaily in the distance. A great siesta would settle over Sydenham Hill, with its large Edwardian houses behind their curving laurel-flanked drives. Outside, in those quiet, too formal gardens, the sun would succeed in penetrating the profuse but tidy shrubberies and the monkey puzzle trees, but in the empty, elegant billiard room there was a perpetual dim diffusion broken only by the sudden stabs of sunlight that shot straight to the parquet floor; sunlight in which the dust flecks danced and floated, to settle eventually on some surface from which, next morning, the inevitable feather duster would send them flying, swirling through space once more in an endless, meaningless repetition.

There were some photographs, carefully posed and framed, near the top of the stairs at Kensington Gore, which seemed to have captured the whole spirit of that remote period. They were taken one afternoon, at the time when my grandfather's large and various family was growing up, and they show, with a yellowing patina of decomposition, long vistas of undisturbed rhododendrons with, here and there, in cunningly contrived niches, the sightless eyes and judiciously broken limbs of statuary protruding coyly from the semi-concealment of the bushes, while in the foreground of each, frozen for all time in some spiritless game of catch or fondling a pet dog, were two pasty little girls in white dresses and black stockings. Seeing them one longs to run through that dark, quiet garden shouting; to hack down those rank and soot-infested shrubs; to turn the hose upon those snail-smeared statues and to tell those poor, dyspeptic little girls to eat more fruit and less starch.

To visit this part of the world now is like walking through catacombs of the dead. One walks down wide roads between houses that seem to be peopled by rich, forgotten ghosts. Here is preserved, more or less intact but for a broken fence, a rotting gateway, the earthly remains of those German business men of the

Edwardian period who made this district a little Fatherland. Here, behind lodge gates, down drives grown green with neglect, stand the seedy mansions of a past generation, as pompous as a Sargent portrait, as absurd as a hobble skirt. After the upheaval of the last war the stream of wealth and fashion shifted its bed and Sydenham Hill was forgotten, for the connoisseur an unrivalled example of Edwardian opulence in galloping decay. Now jays screech undisturbed in the shrubberies or streak across the lawns from one bank of bushes to the next, and it takes but little imagination to believe that one hears the crunching of gravel as the carriages arrive with guests for a musical evening, or a new-fangled motor-car splutters unconvincingly, dropping pools of grease on the drive. Then, as the great drawing-room windows light up once again, the noise of social clamour, swishing silk, chairs drawn back over the parquet floor, and then, in comparative silence, Elgar's "Salut d'Amour" scraped upon the violin.

Through this long Sunday afternoon my grandfather walked, top hatted, frock coated, carrying his hymn book on his way to hand round the bag in church. The garden was even quieter than usual, because he would not allow croquet on Sundays in case the click of the balls should disturb the afternoon rest of his neighbours. This and my grandmother's dictum:

"Don't make a passage through the drawing-room, dears," seems to have been the only unbreakable rule of the household. He was a little preoccupied in those days, his mind still full of some business complication. 'Overheads', 'turnover', 'capital' and 'interest' would be whirling round beneath the silk hat as he walked down the asphalt path which curved, with an artlessness that Nature could not hope to rival, towards the gate at the bottom of the orchard.

There was not the full Pickwickian joviality that came upon him later as he walked down the Row in Hyde Park or examined the first crocuses in Kensington Gardens in that most beatific of all hours to a happy, God-fearing man, the hour between church and Sunday dinner. There was a peculiar attribute of sunniness about the sunshine one met with on coming out of cellar-like coolness of church, which formal Sunday clothes seemed to accentuáte. My grandfather would shuffle down the neat walks of Kensington Gardens, his top hat winking happily in the sun, clicking his false teeth slightly and humming under his breath one of the hymns from the morning service.

I can see him clearly, a small black figure with his head slightly on one side, stumping along much slower than the general stream of traffic, jostled by prams, menaced by fairy cycles, but beaming alike on everyone. Or I see him sitting on a seat beside the

Row, blinking in the strong light, nodding to a friend here, raising his hat there, for he was unaffectedly pleased to see everybody and he always used to say, in his rare moments of profanity: "It's just as easy to say 'Good morning, how are you?' as it is to say 'Damn your eyes.'"

CHAPTER THREE

THE BLUE-SPOTTED WAISTCOAT

Each day in the week has a special quality that is all its own and, I firmly believe, if one could be dropped at random in Time, as one could be dropped from a balloon into space, the really discerning connoisseurs of such delicate niceties could tell, merely from outward appearance, whether they had landed on a Thursday, a Monday or a Saturday. There is a busy, bustling look about Saturday morning that is unmistakable. Then my grandfather would rub his

29

hands briskly after his cold bath in anticipation of a happy day. But for sixty years of his life Wednesday was the apogee of each week, for every Wednesday in winter my grandfather went hunting. In consequence of this, Wednesday, to me, is a day of log fires and drawn blinds, of stiff hands stretched out to warm and of steaming tumblers set beside an empty armchair.

If my grandfather was genial at normal times, on Wednesday evenings, as he stood with his back to a blazing fire, dressed in breeches, black socks, white stock and blue-spotted waistcoat, he was almost overpowered by his love of mankind in general and the whole room seemed permeated with a rosy, cosy, Dingly Dell sort of atmosphere.

In earlier days, when his good nature was more a matter of speculation, his family could depend upon the softening influence of Wednesday evening and it was then, as he drank his sherry and ate his dozen oysters—for, when they were in season, oysters were as much a part of Wednesday as the top hat and hymn book were of Sunday—that they would stand behind his chair and ask, as casually as possible, if they might buy a bicycle or arrange a dance and, in the fullness of his Wednesday evening heart, he would say: "Yes, my dear, of course you may. Certainly, certainly." And he would pour himself out another glass of sherry, his stubby red hands shaking slightly with the exertions of the day and the relaxations of the evening.

The only subject which taxed even Wednesday's powers of amelioration was marriage. Though he advocated early marriages for all, especially young men, on the grounds that it was a steadying influence, and though he had been married young and enjoyed fifty years of complete happiness, for some reason these theories did not seem to apply to his own daughters. His sons he did not seem to mind about. Young men, apparently, could become engaged when and how they liked, but not young women—especially if they happened to be his daughters. On one occasion he shocked his whole family by announcing in a loud voice at dinner: "If another man comes after one of my daughters I'll shoot him." But this threat, though apparently never carried out, was not made upon a Wednesday. Then, if one of his daughters was imprudent enough to show him her new ring, he would merely turn his head sideways, as he did when avoiding a disagreeable subject, and say: "I don't want to see it, my dear", fill his mouth with another oyster and the subject would be closed—at any rate until after Wednesday.

The pack that my grandfather followed for over sixty years hunted in Essex and in early days he would drive to Liverpool Street station from south London in his phaeton. This meant starting at a chilly hour in the morning when the horses stamped and snorted, with white breath sprouting from their nostrils, and old Bob Smith on the box, his hair curling up under his hat brim like a creeping plant, was muffled to the chin in many capes, scarves and great coats. The whole house would be disturbed. The servants would be down early and a special breakfast cooked which my grandfather, in the spotted waistcoat and white stock, would eat in silence and alone, while outside Lucy would be fussing over his flask, repolishing the top for the fourth time or brushing his silk hat, muttering all the time to herself: "Well, I dunno, I'm sure. Well, 'tis be 'opes 'e gets back safe, that's all I can say. But if anythink should 'appen—but, oh well, there 'tis. We've all got to go sometime, I suppose."

Driving through the early morning streets, sitting on the box beside old Bob, my grandfather's head would gradually clear itself of the week's accumulation of business intricacies. Under the benignant influence of Wednesday morning he would blossom from a prosperous Pooterism into a racy Jorrocks or Pickwick as he jogged and swayed up the Seven Sisters Road with his hands plunged into the rugs provided by Lucy. Latterly, though the outward trappings were different, though the journey started from Kensington instead of Sydenham or Peckham and it was undertaken in a prosaic limousine instead of the more romantic phaeton with my grandfather sitting beside Parsons, the chauffeur, and not old Bob Smith, the spirit of Wednesday morning remained constant and ineradicable. In fact it grew, as the contrast between this day with its promise of a world smelling of horses and leather, a world of red faces and blue-spotted waistcoats, with the petrol fumes and dictaphones with which my grandfather was so incongruously surrounded at other times, heightened its peculiarity.

Wednesday at Kensington, as I remember it, was a day of concealed anxiety. My grandfather had ridden since he was a child without any serious accidents, so there is reason to suppose that he was at least a prudent horseman. But there remained the same doubt in everybody's mind—perhaps this day, at last, would be the one to bring trouble. After his seventieth year, naturally, the secret fears of the household increased and my grandmother openly declared that he should give it up. But grandfather, who was both stubborn and evasive on all such really important matters, always managed to put her off with a few vague, insincerely regretful remarks about it being his last season and that next year he really would be too old—though in his own mind he had no intention of giving up while he could still stand.

On Wednesday, then, after the car, with my grandfather, top hatted once more and beaming like a child beside Parsons, with his long, pale face so exactly the opposite of my grandfather's round, red one, had slid out of sight and the front door clanked to, the household would relapse into uneasiness and irritability. My grandmother, who was always too proud to show her agitation, especially in front of The Aunts, would relieve her feelings at the expense of Aunt Pem, whose laughter would become feverish in her anxiety to please, or of Lucy, who spent Wednesdays shaking her head and muttering her expectation of disaster at the front windows, as though the fatal telegram, or better still the ambulance itself, were just round the corner.

On the very rare occasions when my grandfather did meet with a slight accident and arrived home plastered with mud and scratched about the hands and face Lucy would be in her element. "Well there!" she would say to my mother with a bitter laugh. "Well there! You may think me funny, ma dear, but I can't 'elp but laugh because it's only just broke in on my thoughts as you might say. Well there, I was only saying to Ellen this morning, as I was scrubbing the kitchen table—Of course I don't 'ave to scrub the kitchen table, as you know, but it's these 'young girls'. Really they are a pathetic treat, though I don't like to say it—not that I mind the work, of course, I don't want you to think that, ma dear—as you know I never was one to mind what I turned my 'and to and yer mother always says: 'Well, Lucy,' she says, 'there's one thing about it you never was one to make difficulties.' That's what yer mother always says and —Well, as I was saying, I only said to old Ellen this morning: 'Well,' I said, ''Tis be 'opes nothink 'asn't 'appened to 'im because, believe it or not,' I said, 'I've 'ad sich a feeling 'ere all day,' " and she would lay her hand on the pit of her stomach and pause before she continued: " 'Oh, Luce, you old bag of misery,' old Ellen says. But there, I knew somethink 'ad 'appened because it was jest sich a feeling as I 'ad that year I took Mr. Harry to Freshwater. Well, p'raps you wouldn't remember because it was before you was born . . ." And so she would go on, slipping backwards over a compass of forty years in a sentence, then pulling herself with an effort back to the present, only to slither down the slippery slope of reminiscence once more, her face creased with recollection of innumerable domestic tragedies, so many attacks of mumps and scarlet fever, such a quantity of bicycle accidents.

While the too feminine atmosphere of the house at Kensington was charged with the accumulated undercurrents of many years, my grandfather was cantering through the keen air of Epping Forest or waiting silently at some dripping covert-side for that most stirring and elemental of all sounds, the sudden baying of hounds in a hollow wood and the noise of the horn.

However much one may disapprove of hunting on humanitarian grounds or despise it for social reasons as the last refuge of an effete plutocracy, or however much one may laugh in secret at the smug little fraternity of fox hunters with their beefsteak faces and all too simple minds, these intellectual scruples are swept aside in an instant at the first yelping, bubbling, boiling of hounds in a wood and the urgent horn, the bustle, the shouting, the sudden, blood-tingling activity of the field. The flimsy structure of humanitarianism, so laboriously acquired, collapses, as usual, like the walls of Jericho at the first blast of the blood-thirsty hunting horn. All the teachings, the theories of a thousand years are blown away in a second by the most elemental instinct of all —the instinct to kill.

Not that my grandfather, smiling genially on fox or hound alike, or any of the other normal, civilized ladies and gentlemen who were out with him, ever thought of it in this way as they galloped so gloriously over plough and through muddy woodland paths, or clattered home, chatting over the day's experiences, down darkening lanes in an air grown crisp with frost while a great, sad November sun sank below the tree tops. There was no trace of cruelty in my grandfather's cherubic face or in the weatherbeaten countenance of his life-long friend and hunting companion, Sam Fitch, whom my grandfather delighted to describe as "a mere lad of some eighty years" and who, if my grandfather was like Mr. Pickwick in appearance and character, would have served as an excellent model for John Bull himself.

Old Mr. Fitch was the tutelary god of Wednesday; the warm spirit of Wednesday incarnate. For sixty years he and my grandfather had hacked home together on Wednesday evenings, warmed to the very heart with the day's sport and the knowledge that there was a hot bath waiting for them at Mr. Fitch's farmhouse near Epping, and that there would be boiled eggs for tea.

Sitting in front of the roaring fire, after a bath, with the exquisite glow of fatigue in their limbs, my grandfather and Mr. Fitch would renew their weekly friendship. In such a hothouse of good feeling as this it is no wonder that they should have remained the closest of friends over such a long period. It would be hard, after a day in the open air followed by a hot bath and two eggs boiled exactly to your own specifications, to quarrel with even the most diabolical character, and there was nothing at all satanic about these two extremely genial old gentlemen as they sat, eating a large tea, spluttering a little with their eggs and talking with their mouths a little too full.

"Been to any more of those 'set-tos' lately, Richard?" old Mr. Fitch would say in his brusque, John Bullish manner. In the sixty years during which they had been friends Mr. Fitch's fortunes had remained much the same, while my grandfather, battling in the sophisticated world of commercial London, had risen to social heights that seemed dizzy in Epping, and there had grown up between them a feeling that was partly respect for my grandfather's increased wealth— the kind of respect that a schoolboy feels for a friend who has been chosen to play for the first eleven—and partly a feeling, in Mr. Fitch, of pride and vicarious pleasure in my grandfather's new eminence. A speech at a public dinner, a big wedding, or distinguished new acquaintance made in the Row, at a board meeting or at the Court of Petty Sessions where my grandfather was a magistrate, was felt as almost as much of a triumph in Epping as it was in Kensington Gore.

After Mr. Fitch had swallowed, and repeated his question, my grandfather would pretend to look thoughtful for a moment as though racking his brains to remember such unimportant things, for it would not have done to have had a list of dinners, meetings and social functions too readily on his tongue. It was necessary to the self-respect of both that they should keep up some air of casualness. "No, Sam, no, Sam, I don't think I have," my grandfather would answer, wiping his moustache with his table napkin and staring at the ceiling to help him remember all the various events of the past week. Then he would add, in a voice as humble and unconcerned as he could make it, "Unless you count the Peckham Pension Society dinner at the Charing Cross Hotel and judging at the Van Horse Parade at the Botanical Gardens in Regent's Park." And then he would be pressed into giving an account of each, of who had been present, where he had been sitting, who had been sitting next to him and what they had said.

In judging whether my grandfather was a snob because he enjoyed, and enjoyed describing, his encounters with the more exalted, one must take into account the background of the period in which he lived. For unconscious snobbery is not the true sort. In relation to our own times even the most advanced social reformers of a hundred years ago, by the lukewarmness and the condescension of their reforms, would appear detestable snobs and, no doubt, in a few generations' time the firebrands, the social revolutionaries of our day will appear as pale reactionaries, but they are social revolutionaries just the same.

Snobbishness, like its opposite, is relative and must be judged as such—at least as a vice. For a man to be considered a snob in my grandfather's youth he would have had to descend to depths of social repulsiveness unimaginable now, so, if my grandfather's harmless delight in minor titles, his admiration of public pompousness, seems a little strange, one must remember that among his contemporaries he was unusually democratic and, by any standards, unquestionably humble. In fact there was something ingenuous and disarming in this attitude of respect, even though it may seem to us somewhat misplaced.

Driving back to London through the crowded, lamp-lit streets of the northern suburbs my grandfather's head would nod over his evening paper and his chin drop down on to the blue-spotted waistcoat. Alone with Parsons, who was his good friend, he could give way. If he felt tired he could show it. But as soon as the car drew up at Kensington Gore he was confronted with a whole battery of feminine eyes, as searching as arc-lights, that would scan his face for the slightest sign of fatigue. He would step jauntily out of the car, smiling broadly to reassure the eager faces pressed against the study and drawing-room windows. Was he wet? Was he unusually muddy? Had he had a fall? Even Aunt Maria, who had been saying: "Is Richard in yet, Sophy?" until my grandmother could not bear saying "No" any more and had gone downstairs in disgust, would rise from her Patience table at the sound of the car door and make her way slowly, brushing aside such light objects as chairs or small tables with the blind, unswerving purposefulness of an old, black tram, to the drawing-room window, where she could watch my grand-father's triumphal progress from the car to the front door.

The news of my grandfather's arrival seemed to sweep through the house as though by telepathy. Jonzen, the Swedish parlourmaid (who, when she thought nobody was looking, would throw burning matches one after another on to an unlit fire to save herself the bother of stooping), would come bustling out of the privacy of her pantry to open the front door, Aunt Pem would show her relief at the drawing-room window by laughing until her face was twisted up like a crying baby's, and Lucy, with some sewing in her hand and her forehead furrowed with care, would mutter: "Oh well, 'e 'as come back then," with a note of bewilderment in her voice, for she was unable to visualize a safe and happy conclusion to any undertaking, even so slight a one as running out to post a letter at the top of Queen's Gate. Her eyes would watch his every movement as he jumped out of the car and waddled jauntily up the path to the front door to discover the slightest trace of a limp, and she suspected his most unconsidered gesture as having been designed specially to disguise some hidden strain or broken bone. Then her eye would light on something wrong and her voice, rising several octaves, would become almost hysterical. "Well there, 'e 'asn't got 'is warm gloves! Tst, tst! And I put them out specially on the 'all table, that I do know because Ellen was standing just as it might be there when your mother came out of the study and said: 'Oh, Luce, just run and do sech a thing,' I forget now what it was, but I remember as well as anythink putting those warm gloves down beside 'is 'at. Well, if it's that young Ivy put them away again I shan't 'alf 'ave somethink to say to 'er. By gums, I shall 'ave to speak to 'er old fashioned, I shall really. Well, as I tell yer mother, it's not a thankful offer 'aving to train the 'young girls' these days, it really isn't. Well, I don't know what yer puppa will think 'aving to go off like that without 'is warm gloves, because I never was one to forget anythink like that, as you know, and yer puppa always says: 'Well, Lucy,' 'e says, 'you spoil me, you know.' That's what 'e always says. Well, I shall come in after dinner and tell yer puppa that if 'is 'ands was cold it was nothink to do with me— that's all I can say." And she would hobble off out of the room and upstairs, still muttering to herself.

At the long drawing-room window Aunt Pem would laugh until my grandfather was out of sight below the little balcony with its few dank window boxes, and Aunt Maria, having waited stolidly until she heard the front door close safely behind him, would turn and set a rigid course back to her Patience table. Only my grandmother, at the front door, the person to whom his safe arrival mattered most, would have the wisdom to disguise her relief a little and to avoid fussing round him in a too feminine display of welcome.

After a dinner in which, mellowed by fatigue, sherry and oysters, my grandfather could listen to the laughter of Aunt Pem and the curt statistics of Aunt Maria with something very near the loving-kindness that he felt for all the rest of the world, he would sit by the study fire, still in the blue-spotted waistcoat, but with his coat now changed for a velvet smoking jacket, in a blissful Wednesday evening reverie.

CHAPTER FOUR

"TAKE A DOZEN EGGS"

IN the centre of my grandfather's breakfast table there was a silver egg-stand. It was circular with a handle in the middle, and the eggs in silver cups, surmounted by egg cosies made of flannel in the shape of chicken's heads, stood like sentinels round the outside. It was always put in the middle of the table, fully charged with boiled eggs, where it waited patiently to humour some gastronomic whim which never came; for there were always at least two other hot dishes on the sideboard, both of which were more attractive than boiled eggs. But in spite of that the egg-stand was never missing from the table and none of its eight or so cups ever appeared to be empty. It was like a religious emblem or some fetish of a simple race, put there as a sign of Prosperity, to the confusion of the evil spirit of Want, and its presence on the breakfast table was taken for granted by everybody just as much as my grandfather's own shining face as he came through the door after his cold bath and morning ride, clicking his false teeth and humming "O Rest in the Lord."

At lunch and dinner time the fetish would be there again, only this time the gods would be propitiated with custard instead of boiled eggs. There, on the middle of the table or discreetly waiting on the sideboard, would be another silver stand fully loaded with glasses. This was no mass-produced custard made from a powder, but the real thing, full of eggs. Sometimes it was plain, sometimes chocolate flavoured and sometimes coffee, but this variation was merely an academic distinction, a gesture, because its fate, whatever its flavour, was always the same. Jonzen, the stertorous Swedish parlourmaid, would come round to each diner in succession, as though by holding the silver stand by his left ear and muttering an inaudible formula of words he would receive spiritual benefit, then return it to the sideboard where the glasses would stand, humble and forgotten, like those supernumerary flunkeys at a banquet who stand in dark corners merely waiting for someone to drop something.

The only occasion on which the egg-stand was put to use was when my grandfather had one of his younger grandchildren staying with him. Then it was always followed by the "Boiled Egg Game", in which my grandfather delighted almost as much as the child. After the egg was eaten my grandfather would pretend to become absorbed in his paper and, with much whispering and ill-suppressed excitement, the empty shell would be put upside down in the cup and covered with a cosy. As soon as this was done my grandfather would bang his paper down on the table and say: "Well, my boy, what I'd like now would be a nice boiled egg." And, entering into his part as though he had never been through the familiar ritual before, he would examine the egg-stand closely as though trying to decide which one to take. This was a moment of supreme excitement. Would he fall into the trap and take the empty one or would he spoil it all by taking one of the others? Everyone round the table would watch him tensely and my grandfather, obviously enjoying the performance himself, would heighten the excitement by pretending to take the wrong one, and sometimes the child would crack under the strain and, breaking all the conventions of

46

reality, cry out: "No, no, Grandfather, not that one!"
But whether this happened or not, my grandfather
would appear to change his mind at the last minute
and take the right one, saying, with a greedy anticipation that made the inevitable dénouement all the
better: "Ah now! This looks to me like the biggest."
It was an excellently built-up climax, going from one
palpitating situation to another until the greatest
moment of all when my grandfather lifted the cosy
and cracked the empty shell with his spoon.

I firmly believe that no child was ever taken in by
my grandfather's deception any more than he was by
theirs. But that did not make the agony any less when
he seemed about to take the wrong egg, nor did it
make any less delightful the grand climax when his
greediness was punished and he threw up his hands
and pretended to burst into tears. There was a mutual
understanding between them. If one would stick to
the rules and pretend to be deceived, so would the
other. After all, nobody believes that Hamlet is real,
and the actors know that the audience can see through
their little deceptions, but no one gives the show
away. Ophelia goes irritatingly mad on Monday,
Tuesday, and possible twice on Wednesday. Anyone
can find her out, but they come and see her go
through it all again. It was the same with my grandfather and the boiled egg.

47

As his grandchildren grew older even this rare use of the egg-stand ceased, but the stand itself with its load of patient eggs in their cockerel cosies remained the same. If the custom had been discontinued a feeling of deep uneasiness would have spread round the family just as it did when, after he was seventy years old, my grandfather suddenly took to marmalade. After a lifetime of jam and honey he changed. What possessed him, I wonder, on this particular morning, to break a habit of taste so long formed and open the marmalade pot after, possibly, fifty years? Perhaps it was springtime and, on his early morning ride in Hyde Park, he had found the first flowers of the horse chestnut unexpectedly open. Perhaps he had smelt for the first time that indefinable smell of a London summer which seems to be made up of blossom, smoky sunshine and hot pavements; or it may have been only a particularly big dividend. At any rate something "shook his frail frame at eve with throbbings of noontide". A spirit of youthful adventure came over him which crystallized itself in the form of marmalade. Not many men, I like to think, after a steady life of conservatism and sobriety, a life in which all material ambitions had been achieved, would have had enough of the old flexibility still in them to take such a step.

The effect on his family was deep. There were

whisperings in the basement and in the parlourmaid's pantry. Letters sped to the married members all over the country. My grandfather, a noted abstainer, had suddenly taken to marmalade. The word flew round. It was a sign, like one of those portentous trifles that precede some great cataclysm of nature. The family waited in suspense. But nothing happened—except that my grandfather continued to eat marmalade.

When breakfast was over and my grandfather had disappeared, clutching *The Times* in one hand and his slip-on glasses with the other, I often wondered what happened to those forlorn eggs. Even in summertime, with salads at every meal, no household, however large and strange, could have found a use for eight hard-boiled eggs a day, to say nothing of the several pints of custard. I hope that they were the same eggs day after day or, better still, china ones like those used to deceive credulous chickens, but I fear that this was very unlikely.

There was an atmosphere of careless plenty about my grandfather's time that amounted, sometimes, to a kind of fatalism. Buying, to my grandmother, was a reflex action quite unrelated to needs. Her progress through a shop was queenly. She had the really vicious shopper's habit of buying first and thinking of a reason afterwards. She bought birthday presents regardless of dates and Christmas presents in May, storing them away in unlikely drawers and wardrobes where they would remain hidden for years, coming to light long after their object had been forgotten. The feeling of fatalism was strong in her, too. When one of her daughters tried to stop her buying oranges by explaining that the last dozen had gone bad she merely said: "Never mind, dear, they'll soon be out of season," and bought another dozen.

Seen from the precarious present this attitude seems a little shocking, like the debauchery of some oriental Croesus, but at the time it seemed natural enough and my grandfather's method of living was generally considered very frugal, for he came from an age when even the bizarre excesses of Mrs. Beeton could be, and were, followed to the letter. It was a period of plethora and baroque, even in cooking, as it was in decoration. Supply was so much greater than demand that the maxim "take a dozen new-laid eggs and a pint of the best cream, beat for half an hour and then throw away" was both possible to carry out and in every way sound economically. Eggs and cream were plentiful and the labour of the beater and the hen was cheap. Life was simple and clear cut; there were no confusing complexities or half-tones. Those who had money could, without a pang of conscience, demand the beating up of eggs and those who had not, without hesitation or a word of criticism, would beat.

It was that blissful lack of conscience which made the late Victorian and Edwardian periods the golden age for the rich. Those were the days of wealth for wealth's sake, when richness was admired, envied and respected by all. Now, rich men, brought up in an atmosphere tinged with unconscious liberalism, creep about the countryside like lepers, jealously hiding their financial deformity. It is reasonable to assume that there is little pleasure left these days in the knowledge that one owns more than anybody should, or in watching the struggles of the less favoured to compete for the honour of supplying one with all the non-essentials of life. Wealth is no longer fashionable and even the comparatively affluent will go to great lengths to prove that they are on the point of bankruptcy and that all their possessions are quite valueless. This is a revolution of considerable importance which has come about in our time and in our midst, with scarcely a word of recognition from anyone. My grandfather's egg-stand, like so many of the eggs it once held, is in the dustbin once and for all.

DENIS CONSTANDUROS.

CHAPTER FIVE

NOISES AND PLACES

WHENEVER I recall my grandfather I think of him chiefly in the evenings. There was something in the comfortable relaxation of the evening, after a busy day, that clearly epitomized my grandfather's character as I remember him. He probably preferred the morning, with its cold bath and ride before breakfast, but I like best to think of him sitting in his arm-chair after a good, though not necessarily large, dinner, puncturing the first cigar of the day with a look of expansive beatitude on his face and "The Times Newspaper" as he always called it—for he came of a generation which also had the leisure and energy to speak of "sherry wine"—folded across his stumpy legs.

In earlier years he would sit up at night and read adventure stories in order to be able to re-tell them to his grandchildren in the morning. When my brother and I were dressing we would hear his sing-song voice calling to us down the long, unlit passages of the house on Sydenham Hill, and we would hurry off to his dressing-room and sit, rapt in attention, while he shaved himself with a cut-throat razor before his old-fashioned shaving stand and told us haltingly, with pauses for shaving, the story of three characters called Ralph, Peterkin and Jack in *The Gorilla Hunters*, or gruesome tales of lions from a book called *The Man-eaters of Tsavo*. Told by my grandfather, still fresh from his cold bath and morning ride, the stories seemed to gain a new actuality that made them far more absorbing and memorable than anything merely read aloud. One always had the feeling that grand-father himself had met one of the notorious man-eaters lurking among the rhododendrons of Dulwich Park.

There is an easy, rather obvious sentimentality about the evening which suited my grandfather and his generation admirably. Those were simple days when a painter could be satisfied with the facile emotionalism of syrup-like sunset or the depiction of old age, and any artist with the dash and courage to include both on the same canvas was almost sure of an admiring crowd at Burlington House. My grandfather might almost be said to have included both in his own person, as his genial red face was like a setting sun and he carried an aura of evening comfort and accomplishment, of glowing fires and placidity with him as naturally as a snail carries its shell.

For that reason my mind slips back most easily to the picture of my grandfather beside the study fire, his short legs stretched out stiffly on to a hassock, like a child who cannot touch the ground, and his gouty fingers fumbling with his after-dinner cigar. The tray with the whiskey and the tonic water, which nobody ever drank, is in position on the study table, as far as possible from my grandfather's chair, and the dull London traffic rumbling by outside the curtained windows with a sound so incessant as to be almost inaudible after a time, like the noise of a waterfall or of the sea to those who live within earshot of them, adding a feeling of security, by contrast, to the comfort of the room. Or perhaps it is a summer evening. My brother and I take it in turns to read aloud *Pickwick Papers* or *The Fortunes of Nigel*; for my grandfather had an unfortunate fondness for the slow-motion romanticism of Scott; and as we read, park keepers in the gardens opposite are beginning to chant: "All out" and toll their hollow hand-bells.

Sitting in the fading light by the study window and following—or failing to follow—the tortuous fortunes of Nigel, the sound had a peculiar quality that stays in the memory. It seems now to be the key to that whole period, something peculiar both to the place and to the time, as the hooting of tugs on the river does to those who have once lived in Chelsea. If it were possible to play back in one's mind a record of those park keepers with the exact intonation of the chanted "All out" and the tolling hand-bells, first from somewhere nearby and then thinly, as a counter theme, an answering shout from far away in the gardens where a white mist is beginning to rise under the trees, I feel that I could recapture one instant of time in the round, instead of flatly, in the two dimensions of memory, and that I could actually hear the splutter of my grandfather's syphon as it emptied or smell the peculiarly dusty smell of the green plush cloth on the study table.

There are other sounds which, to a lesser degree, have the power to evoke the period, such as the shutting of the heavy front door and the sudden diminution of traffic noise which always brought with it the elemental feeling of seclusion and security: of being unassailably remote from the world. Then there was the early morning noise to which one woke. The practice rooms of the Royal College of Music were close behind my grandfather's house and the first sound that one heard on waking up was a babel of trilling sopranos, thumping pianos and scraping violins, a chaotic pattern of scales, repeated phrases and sudden cadenzas that was as thrilling as the tuning-up of an orchestra or as the busy tumult of birds at daybreak and which always gave one an indefinable feeling, as one lay half awake, that the curtain was about to go up on a day full of the promise of good things.

But neither of these so exactly suits the period as the muezzin-like wailing of the park keepers at closing time. I can see my grandfather, a lonely black figure in the encroaching darkness, trotting in complete solitude towards a locked park gate—for the sound of those keepers and the knowledge that the Gardens were closing always roused some imp of perversity in him and he invariably entered the Gardens very slowly, just as everyone else was hurrying to the gates. In a few moments the crowds would melt away, the twisting paths would be empty except for this one figure, moving very slowly and apparently oblivious to everything. The cries of the keepers and the ringing of their hand-bells would begin to sound from all directions like lights snapping on in the darkness, but still he would move on, a solitary figure in a de-populated world, until at last he came to a gate where he would have to tip the porter half a crown to let him out.

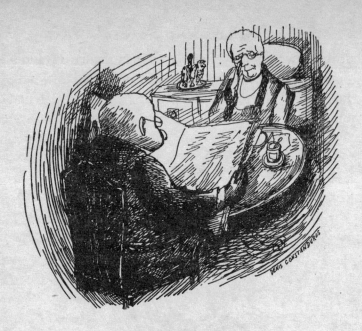

CHAPTER SIX

MY GRANDMOTHER PULLS A FACE

O N the morning of my grandparents' golden
wedding, Lucy, bringing them their early morning cup of tea and the two regulation pieces of thin
bread and butter, greeted them by saying: "Well, I
can't say *many* 'appy returns of the day, I suppose,
but 'tis be 'opes with care—and cheerfulness—we
might say a few."

My grandmother was angry about it because she
did not like being reminded of the fact that she could
not expect many more "happy returns", but grand-

father went off for his early morning ride delighted to have another anecdote to tell his grand new friends in the Row. Their attitude towards age was different, partly, no doubt, because my grandfather's health was always robust, while my grandmother was for many years in that precarious state when one slight illness— a cold not shaken off or an attack of bronchitis—would have made her a permanent invalid. Living in a house with old people has its disadvantages. There are so many topics that cannot be discussed, so very many taboos. One's mind becomes unnaturally agile in anticipating any topic that may lead, however indirectly, to a reference to the future. Merely remembering the past becomes a sterile occupation when it is not accompanied by anticipations of the future.

My grandfather's own attitude to old age was mixed, but when he was over seventy he developed a great personal pride in his own age and was only too eager to tell everybody how old he was. He acquired a record-breaker's outlook and, in order to make himself out as old as possible, even went to the length of adding a year by saying, when he was seventy-five, that he was in his seventy-sixth year. There is a jealous rivalry among the really old. This made things very difficult when dealing with my grandfather, because to mention anyone who was several years older than himself and still active, while it was a

compliment in that it implied that he was comparatively young and had many years before him, was a
mortal insult to his professional pride as an Old Man.
If he was to be old at all, then he would be older
than anybody else.

Sometimes, when he was in the mood to be considered young, he would look down the Deaths
column in "The Times Newspaper" until he came to
the announcement of somebody considerably older
than himself and he would read it out with obvious
satisfaction, starting off with the words: "Well now,
here's a poor young chap cut off in his prime." Then
he would read on gaily: "At Elmbank, Tranmere
Road, Wimbledon Common, Nathaniel Prangle, in
his ninety-third year . . ." And he would take another
piece of toast and marmalade, encouraged by the
thought that, to Nathaniel Prangle, floating about in
the cosmos, he must appear a mere child.

It seems strange that anyone so cheerful, so essentially alive and in full enjoyment of this world as my
grandfather appeared to be after his cold bath and his
morning ride should have breakfasted regularly off
obituary notices. Perhaps it gave him a twinge of
malicious satisfaction while sitting at the breakfast
table, glowing with his recent exercise, and still
experiencing the mundane pleasures of hot tea and
toast too thickly buttered, to read of those who had

failed to remain alive any longer. At any rate he took what appeared to be a morbid interest in the death of anyone he had known, however slightly, and was an eager and conscientious attender of funerals. Breakfast, though it still contrived to be a cheerful meal, as any meal at which my grandfather presided would have been, was always eaten to the accompaniment of a list of names of the recently dead, reverberating round the room like the tolling of a bell.

My grandmother, who probably thought more about death itself, did not share his keen interest in the dead and cut him short one morning in the middle of his reading by saying that she thought it was selfish of old people to die after a long illness. Why couldn't they die before and save their relations all the trouble? Grandfather was disgusted at this frivolous and illogical point of view and from that day onward, whenever he came to the words "after a long and painful illness bravely borne" he would say: "Ah, another selfish chap, I see," with a bitter intake of breath through his white moustache.

Obituary notices were not his only breakfast-table reading. During the Great War he would read at length extracts from *The Times* about the military position. It was a pity for my grandfather, as for many other Englishmen of his generation, that the war was fought in France. Almost any other country would have been better, for he could not bring his Anglo-Saxon lips to form the mincing, emasculate sounds made by Frenchmen. It seemed to him a sign of embarrassing affectation to pronounce French place names correctly so, like his often-quoted friend Mr. Boffen, in his readings of *The Rise and Fall of the Roman Empire* ("the old 'Rise and Fall off the Rooshun?' Why I ain't been right slap through him lately," etc., etc.), he would crash his way through one obstacle and, before he could recover his mental balance, he would be confronted by another. And so he would go on, frequently stumbling, sometimes hesitating and often reduced to using sheer brute force, but never beaten, while my grandmother, sitting at the other side of the table, unseen behind the paper, would make absurd and disrespectful faces at him as a kind of running accompaniment.

If by any mischance he had lowered his paper at the wrong moment and seen those faces he would have been utterly at a loss to understand them. In his own mind he had built up an entirely fictitious character for my grandmother, composed of all that was fine and noble in womanhood, or at any rate all that was considered fine and noble in womanhood during the latter half of last century. To him she was not a mere human being but a Dickens heroine, and who could imagine Dora squinting and putting out her tongue behind David Copperfield's back, however laudable such an action may seem nowadays? But who knows, perhaps Dickens' heroines were human after all, like my grandmother, in their off moments? Even Little Nell, when she was not catching her author's eye, may have given way to some minor vulgarity—at least let us hope so.

The trouble with my grandfather and his contemporaries was over-simplification. To them heroes were perpetually heroic, twenty-four hours in the day, and villains as persistently evil. There were no half tones, no gradations from good to bad. They had a tendency to divide humanity quite simply by two in all matters, whether actual or metaphysical. Their world was conveniently composed of Beauty and Ugliness, Radicals and Conservatives, God and the Devil, Oxford and Cambridge. It was a simple world.

Fortunately for my grandfather he never lowered the paper in time to see those disquieting grimaces, and so he remained, for the fifty-two years in which they lived together, pleasantly and sentimentally ignorant of at least half his wife's character; for those grimaces were significant.

They were significant of my grandmother's rebellion against the humdrum routine of a materially easy life and were part of that curious urge which forced her, during many long summer afternoons, to drive round Surrey looking at houses which she herself knew quite well would never be taken. There were at one time hardly any largish houses within a radius of twenty miles of south London outside which I have not sat with Parsons for many weary hours playing our own specially invented game of cribbage with the number plates of passing cars, while my grandmother, sometimes reluctantly accompanied by grandfather himself, would trail round the garden seeking an unattainable, a non-existent Perfect House. As my grandfather prospered, so these house-hunting Odysseys grew more frequent and less satisfying to my grandmother until, in the words of her family, she could be content with nothing less than a shady desert.

All this was implied in those faces behind the morning paper if my grandfather had but seen them, but he did not. He remained, as I have said, in a state of pleasantly sentimental ignorance until she died. After her death his sentimentality flourished unchecked, though, with a complexity of motive that must have been confusing to himself, his first action was to write to the newsagent and stop the periodicals which my grandmother took and his next was to pay for her funeral out of the money in her banking account. For, though he was obviously overcome by grief and emotion, he was at all times that most un-Dickensian mixture, a practical sentimentalist.

CHAPTER SEVEN

THE GREY BOWLER HAT

ONE evening when my brother was having dinner alone with my grandfather (these *tête-à-tête* dinners, by the way, which they had frequently at the time, were nearly always spoilt by the fact that my grandfather had bought a bottle of orange bitters at Harrods. Someone among his new friends had recommended him to do so and, brought up as he was on sherry and port wine, he drank it in a glass neat, and my brother, out of ignorance and respect, did so too. There was a great fuss made of opening the bottle and taking the first sip. They both drank together and then paused in silence while Jonzen, the Swedish parlourmaid, breathed with gusty obsequiousness in the background. They paused. The drink was nauseating. There was no way out now. It had been recommended by someone who knew what was what, it had been ordered specially from Harrods, brought to the dining-room, examined, opened and tasted in impressive silence. After such a preparatory fanfare there was nothing left but to like it. "Well, my boy," said my grandfather, smiling bravely, "what do you think of it?" What could my brother say? My grandfather refused to be beaten. Every time they were left to dine alone he would say, as though it was a special treat: "Well, my boy, what about a glass of orange bitters?" And each would know, with a heavy heart, that they were condemned to a meal of misery.)

As I was about to say, one night when they were dining alone together my brother suddenly said: "Why don't you buy a grey bowler?" At first my grandfather was dubious about such a break with established precedent, as he had worn nothing but a black silk hat on Sundays—and Wednesdays in the hunting season—or a black bowler on all other days for a long lifetime.

The uninitiated may feel that there is a merely academic distinction between a black bowler and a grey one. Each, they may argue, is a hat. They are identical shapes, even the colour is only a difference of tone. What ignorance! One might as well argue that there is no difference between Beethoven's Choral Symphony and "Pop Goes the Weasel". Each is music, each based on the same fundamental laws of construction, but it would be as impossible for the average black-bowlered city clerk to whistle the Choral Symphony from beginning to end as it would be for him to change his bowler to a grey one. He would not lose his job, no doubt, nor would his wife leave him. The tradesmen, in all probability, would not ask for an immediate settlement of their accounts. In fact, there would be no disastrous consequences, such as those which bring obedience to the laws of man. In spite of this a force far stronger than the threat of imprisonment prevents him performing the simple and quite legal act of buying a grey bowler hat, even if it is his one consuming desire.

It would be useless and tiresome to attempt a learned and pompously scientific explanation of this force, though no doubt it could be done by psycho-pathological research in a mere matter of a few hours and an answer given as neat, as shapely and as tasteless as an algebraic equation. We need go no deeper into the question than to say that it is the force which makes elephants act like elephants and Chinamen like

Chinamen. It is the force which prevents a tram from behaving like a bus, for there are prescribed limits to the actions of individuals which may not be exceeded except by those rare personalities with sufficient strength to break these pre-natal bonds. Obviously anyone with these special qualities would not remain long a city clerk.

Therefore when my grandfather debated the question of buying a grey bowler he was contemplating a far greater step than he realized. Only a man who had had the courage to take to marmalade late in life would have considered it for a moment. For some days the subject was dropped, while my grandfather's imagination toyed with the idea, then, one night after dinner, the decision was taken. He would buy one. Lucy, who always bought his clothes for him—half a dozen shirts at a time, all alike, a box of black or dark blue ties, a dozen pairs of black socks—was sent to the hatters to select a number to be sent on approval. The next evening, when dinner was over, my grandfather and my brother retired to the study in suppressed excitement to try them on. There they lay on the round study table, some in boxes, some in virginal tissue paper: four gleaming, unsullied, seductive grey bowler hats. What a scene it must have been in front of the study fireplace, with my grandfather whistling "O Rest in the Lord" under his breath in an attempt to show that trying on a grey bowler was an everyday matter and scarcely worth a moment's interest.

It is hard to say whether the grey bowler was a symptom or a cause of the change, the expansion, that took place in my grandfather during the last few years of his life. During the period in which he was building his business there was little time to consider whether he had any tastes beyond work, and no time at all to indulge them if he had. But latterly, in the mood induced by the wearing of the grey bowler hat, he developed a keen interest in cricket and the Royal Academy.

He would leave the office slightly early on fine summer evenings and drive, perhaps, to Burlington House, where he had a season ticket, and spend a happy hour in that sedately hushed atmosphere, stumping from room to room with his marked catalogue open, revisiting favourites, pausing here to admire a particularly succulent landscape, and there a flashing equestrian scene. Or he would tell Parsons to drive him to the Oval and they would bowl down the Vauxhall Bridge Road faster than they went towards Piccadilly, because Parsons was a cricket enthusiast himself and if Somerset happened to be the visiting side the rivalry between him and my grandfather became acute.

Inside, on the hard benches of the members' stand, my grandfather would doze through many an hour of contentment while the slow white figures moved to and fro in the smoky sunlight of late afternoon. There is always a pleasant drowsiness about a cricket match towards the end of a long day's play, when desultory applause ripples round the ground like little waves on a hot beach, and though my grandfather was a comparatively new-comer to the Oval and to cricket in general, the mellow atmosphere of the place suited him admirably. He would sit there nodding like any hardened habitué, until some spectacular piece of play —a catch on the boundary or a particularly lusty hit by one of his heroes, for it was in the great days of Surrey cricket, when the side included Hobbs, Sandham, Fender, and Strudwick—roused him to a state of unrestricted enthusiasm that must have branded him at once as a mere amateur of the game. He felt, too, the proper schoolboy veneration for the long refreshment room in the pavilion, with its photographs of the famous and its air of determined ugliness, and for the steps down which so many illustrious boots had clanked on their way to the wicket.

The grey bowler had another, indirect effect also. He took to the theatre. For many years he had not been to anything, but an occasional Oratorio, of which he was extremely fond—in fact, he never missed a performance of "Elijah" or "The Messiah" and kept a kind of score card in his memory of the number of times he had heard them. But the theatre came as something completely new to him. "The Beggar's Opera" became his chief favourite and the Lyric Theatre at Hammersmith was as much his haunt as Burlington House or the Oval, and he would sit in his stall, beating time to the familiar tunes with both his short, gouty hands, like a delighted baby. In fact, my grandfather's whole approach to the theatre was child-like in the extreme. He was so inexperienced a theatre-goer that he came to it with a child's eye and was happily deceived by everything. No conventional phrase was too threadbare and no plot too banal to please him, for he had seen none of them before. He was the perfect audience and, on some occasions, must have exceeded even the wishes or intentions of authors, actors, producers and management, for once, at the end of the second act of a musical comedy, when the heroine in a white frock stood among the cardboard clematis to sing a routine sentimental number about the apparent faithlessness of her lover, my grandfather, who could not bear to see a woman unhappy, especially after dinner, burst into tears.

CHAPTER EIGHT

"A FEW OUGHTS"

SOME of my grandfather's quotations from Dickens were developed and amplified into the form of small dramatic performances in which the whole table took part and gave their allotted responses. There was one special favourite from *Pickwick Papers* which went, as far as I can remember, like this:

MY GRANDFATHER (*pouring himself out another glass of sherry*): "What was the last thing you dewoured?" says the doctor.

MY BROTHER: "Roast beef", says the patient.

MY GRANDFATHER (*pausing with the glass in his hand*): "What arter that?" says the doctor.

MYSELF: "Crumpets", says the patient.

MY GRANDFATHER: "That's it," says the doctor.

MY BROTHER: "What's it?'' says the patient.

MY GRANDFATHER (*through the sherry glass*): "Crumpets," says the doctor.

MY BROTHER: "But crumpets is 'olesome," says the patient.

MY GRANDFATHER (*banging down his empty glass*): "Crumpets is *not* 'olesome," says the doctor, wery fierce.

This was the *bon bouche* we had all been waiting for. It never failed to bring the house down and was the juiciest line in the whole performance. My grandfather put all he knew into those stirring words, "Crumpets is *not* 'olesome," and I can hear his chuckle of satisfaction now after "wery fierce", as he beamed round the table in the dull glow of the lamp from the sideboard. It did not matter in the least that we had been through the whole performance the evening before and would undoubtedly do so again the next day. In fact there is something comforting about repetition for its own sake, especially to the ingenuous and unwary, as all concocters of propaganda, from religion to politics, know. The human mind takes kindly to repetitions. One has only to say a thing often enough and the critical faculties, lulled by the tom-tom-like rhythm of sound, will accept it without a murmur. The very fact that my grandfather had said those words so many times before made them seem part of his daily life and one of his necessary comforts, like the glass of whisky and the after-dinner cigar.

In spite of his bold decision to buy a grey bowler and his taking to marmalade my grandfather was at heart a confirmed ritualist. He rose at the same hour every morning and trotted off to his cold bath, dressed in long pants which made him look more like Mr. Pickwick than ever, and at exactly the same moment every day he would cross the road and mount his horse from the mounting block just inside Kensington Gardens.

He was greatly helped in all this by Lucy. She was an arch ritualist. Whenever my grandfather went away for a holiday, which was as seldom as he could manage, she would arrange his room to be as nearly a replica of his study at home as she could make it: an arm-chair, with *The Times* folded over one arm, would be placed at the same angle to a smoking table as his chair at home. In fact everything would be done to make him forget that he had gone away at all. This was largely to shield him from shock, which, to Lucy, was inseparable from all forms of change and extremely dangerous to the system. Therefore change, in any form, was a thing to be avoided at all costs. (That was why, as I have said, she removed the purple bath mat from my grandfather's bathroom. It was replaced with one the colour of quiet mud.)

The satisfaction that my grandfather felt, then, when he declaimed the words: " 'Crumpets is *not* 'olesome,' says the doctor, wery fierce," was a good, natural and primitive feeling. It was much the same as a native craftsman must feel after having repeated the same pattern for the five hundred and sixty-fourth time or a priest on uttering a familiar formula of words.

It was the number of times he said it that pleased him. There is always something mesmeric in high numbers, as my grandfather knew himself, for, if he happened to glance through one of the less-sober newspapers which occasionally found their way on to the breakfast table, and saw a lurid headline such as "50,000,000 Die in World's Most Terrible Tornado", or some other soothing story of other people's troubles, he was not taken in for a moment. "Chah!" he would say, putting down the paper in disgust, "What are a few oughts to a newspaper man?" and he would revert to his *Times*, which would put the whole cataclysm in its place by merely mentioning it on an unimportant page, among meteorological reports, as "High Wind Velocity Recorded in Parts of Patagonia".

The mesmerism of high numbers is perfectly illustrated in Military Tattoos. Huge crowds will come from great distances in the middle of the night to see a thousand men doing at once what nobody would walk across the road to see one man do by himself. If one man wants to swing an Indian club that is his own business and nobody will be sufficiently interested even to try to stop him, but if a thousand men should swing Indian clubs together, then large sums can be charged for the pleasure of seeing them. A thousand times nought—or as my grandfather would have said "ought"—is not "ought", as any newspaper man knows, but about a million.

CHAPTER NINE

THE RICHMOND HORSE SHOW

SOME time in June the Richmond Horse Show was held and the Coaching Club met at the Powder Magazine beside the Serpentine. In my recollection it was always the sunniest day of the year, though this may be because, for some unknown reason, it was to me one of the most exciting. Whether my memory has succeeded in editing the facts and excluding all occasions on which the Coaching Meet was held in the rain or whether the explanation is simply that we did not go when it was wet I cannot say. I only know that every time I cross the bridge over the Serpentine and pass the low, pleasing exterior of the Magazine I am transported into a world of sunshine and new paint, of stamping horses and clinking harness: a world in which all the women wear new summer dresses and the men carnations in their buttonholes. All, that is, except me.

The day of the Coaching Marathon was always a great one for the household at Kensington Gore. For days before Lucy would be preparing my grandfather's clothes, pressing and ironing, muttering to herself like a soul in torment, brushing his silk hat and then replacing it in its white box on the top of the cupboard in the downstairs cloakroom, where it would be safe from the infidel hands of the "young girls". "Well there, 'tis be 'opes no one don't touch 'is 'at because 'e always likes me to get 'is things ready for 'im, that I do know. 'E always did say: 'Lucy,' 'e says, 'there's no one can get a shine on a silk 'at like you can,' 'e says. I can remember 'im saying that as well as anythink many years ago. Well, it must 'ave been a long time ago because I was just as it might be here on the stairs, taking up Mr. Reggie's tray with 'im in bed with the chicken-pox—or was it when Miss Marjory 'ad whooping cough? Tst! Well there, I forget. No, it couldn't 'ave been Miss Marjory because that was the year yer granny took the 'ouse at 'Ind'ead. Oh, that was a nice 'ouse! As soon as I saw it I said: 'Well there! That's what I call a really nice 'ouse.' I don't mean ter say that yer granny didn't always take nice 'ouses. She always took the best and that we know, but that little 'ouse at 'Ind'ead was sweet pretty . . ." And her voice would trail on to an invisible audience when one was two flights up the stairs.

On the great day itself there was a special quality even about the noise from the practice rooms of the Royal College. I am sure that, lying in bed with one's back to the window in the half-conscious stage between sleeping and waking, one could tell from the thrilling cadenzas of the violins, the sudden cascade of notes from the pianos and the exuberant contraltos that it was a sunny morning and that something un-usually good was to happen during the day. It was one of those days when the most familiar sounds, taxis hooting, the grinding of buses as they started away from the bus stop across the road, all seemed charged with a special significance, were all part of a pattern of sound, an overture to great things.

Downstairs the activity was tremendous. Sand-wiches were being spread and cut, meat pies packed in greaseproof paper and the inevitable bottles of tonic water and ginger ale, as well as something stronger for my grandfather himself and any of his distinguished friends who might be entertained, squeezed into picnic baskets that were an excitement in themselves. (Anybody who can resist the sight of a well-filled picnic basket and all it implies is, I solemnly state, dead to this world and ripe for the next.) Jonzen hurried in and out of her pantry on mysterious errands connected with bottles and glasses. In the basement Ellen, with sleeves rolled up and, probably, a glass of stout under a dish cover, was directing operations among "the young girls", while Lucy ran to and fro between them all, up and down stairs, pressing, polishing, cutting, packing, fitting in, pulling out: in fact, performing every domestic feat known to woman, all within the space of a few moments and all with a face seamed with woe and a voice two octaves higher than usual to mark the importance of the occasion.

The arrangement for the day was that we should all congregate at the Magazine in the morning to see the Meet and to watch the coaches start. When the last one had gone we should drive down to Richmond with Parsons in time to see them arrive. My grandfather, who acted as an umpire, went down on one of the coaches while we, with the lunch basket, hurried on to get there first.

It was a fine sight at eleven o'clock on those June mornings in front of the Powder Magazine. It was too early in the day and too early in the year to be really

hot. The sun did not beat up from the asphalt pavements with the vitiating power of late July or August
and the new green of the trees was not yet dulled
and dishevelled by the dust of a long London summer.
Everything was new, fresh and full of promise.
Everything perhaps, except the odd, horsey old
gentlemen in their grey top hats and their shepherd's
plaid trousers. Neither they nor their anachronistic
pastime were either new or particularly fresh, except
in glinting paint and brass, and certainly not full of
promise. Indeed, it would have been hard to find a
more completely lost cause or a more hopelessly
irrelevant gathering of human beings in the country
than those buttonholed old gentlemen and their
elegant, exquisite women. Fortunately for me I was
able, in those days, to look on them in a spirit of
detachment. My eye was unclouded by the cataract of
a social conscience and, in my ignorance, I was able
to enjoy the spectacle for what it was worth. I enjoyed
it with the simplicity of a baby or an artist, for to
each it is the appearance of a thing that matters; its
shape, colour, sound and smell. There are not a whole
dead weight of consequences and implications
attached, like weeds round a swimmer's legs, to
everything seen. They are more interested in the
colour of a thing than its price, how it was made,
who made it and how much per hour they were paid

to do so. At least they should be, for if they are not they are no longer babies—or artists.

We arrived at the Meet, I think, separately from my grandfather. This was to be his day. As an umpire and the owner of a coach, though it was the property of his business and not privately owned like the very best coaches, he was so exalted and so greatly superior to the rest of the family that we came humbly by ourselves, not daring to catch his eye or to look as though we might belong to him as he stood out in the middle of the road among the fine horses and the strange, ramshackle old gentlemen who seemed so impressively distinguished when viewed from the respectful distance of the kerb. There he stood in the middle of it all, smiling on everybody, exchanging a word here and there with someone whose picture one had seen in the society papers, while we, watching from the less-colourful crowd on the pavement, pretended, if he should turn our way, to be very busy looking in another direction, so that he should be spared the embarrassment of having to acknowledge us. There was a tacit agreement between us, like the arrangement between brothers at school, that we should not take advantage of our connection or presume sufficiently to expect recognition, but I can remember hoping secretly that he would come over to the kerb in his splendid horsey clothes with his membership badge dangling from the lapel of his coat, and say just a few words so that we should be elevated above the rest of the crowd pressing round us or, better still, that some gilded gentleman from the box seat of one of the coaches might recognize us as his relations and raise an exquisite hat.

Generally my grandfather would come across to see us and sometimes even introduced us to one of his friends, for an acquaintance in the Row had reported favourably upon us, but if by chance or design he failed to see us in the crowd I was reduced to seeking out the business coach and making myself known to old Bob Smith, the coachman, who, as a lifelong employee of my grandfather's was bound to touch his hat respectfully.

At eleven o'clock there would be a general stir among the knowledgeable and privileged few and among the coaches drawn up on either side of the road. An especially gorgeous gentleman would begin running up and down the road, calling out, gesticulating, ushering away the crowd and, amid the clicking of tongues and unrhythmical stamping of hoofs, the first coach would rumble into movement. Everybody would stand back and cast appraising eyes over the turnout. The driver would raise his whip with a flourish, in every direction hats would be tilted and the guard would rise in his seat and blow a brave, triumphant fanfare. The sun shone and glinted on new paint and polished brass, on silk hats and summer dresses as the first coach rattled magnificently away over the bridge across the Serpentine and was lost in the traffic.

The starter would look at his watch and, after a few minutes, the whole process would begin again, and so on, until the last coach had rumbled into the distance and the space in front of the Magazine seemed emptier than ever before. Then the crowd would disperse until there were only a few nurses with perambulators or groups of children with tiddlers in a jam jar and we would walk home again through a park humming with the gathering momentum of a summer day.

This, though possibly the best part, was only the beginning of the day's activities. There was the drive down to Richmond, beside Parsons, the arrival on the ground and the excitement of finding one's allotted parking place, and then, on getting out of the car beside the judging ring, that peculiar smell of trampled grass and hot humanity which transports one instantly into a world of race meetings and Bank Holidays. There we would sit, eating the superabundance of sandwiches, patties and salads, while a seemingly endless succession of horses trotted, cantered, galloped or merely walked round the ring to the sound of "Light Cavalry", or "The Blue Danube" from a military band in the centre.

I do not know why this day should have had such a fascination for me at all other times of the year. I did not ride and knew nothing about horses. As the long afternoon dragged by and the meaningless succession of horses paraded round the ring or waited for what seemed hours before the judges, I would sit in the car in my unsuitably stiff clothes, while the upholstery of the seats became so hot that one could not bear to touch it. Gradually, as I drowsed in the front seat of the car and the noise of the band, fluctuating with the distance, came in intermittent gusts of sound, I experienced the annual disillusionment that this was, after all, an exceptionally boring day. It was like the yearly disappointment of Christmas, which I always looked forward to all the year round. It was not until it actually came that I experienced once again that peculiarly seasonal ennui which reminded me that Christmas was no longer what it used to be. Sitting in the car through the long afternoon I would have the feeling that this year the magic of the Horse Show had failed to work, that I was growing blasé and unable to enjoy things as I used. It was not until some years later that I realized there never had been any magic.

DENIS CONSTANDUROS.

CHAPTER TEN

"IS" OR "BE"?

At the end of the dark downstairs passage of the
house in Kensington Gore, near the little boxroom
in which my grandfather's silk hat was kept, along
with such miscellaneous objects as old riding boots,
a shooting stick, pictures with broken glass and,
occasionally, copies of Punch piled up on curtained
shelves waiting eternally to be bound, was a small
cloakroom. In this cloakroom there was a notice, in
my grandfather's spiky, Victorian handwriting, on a

post card, yellow and curling with age, which said:

"PLEASE HOLD DOWN UNTIL CISTERN
BE EMPTY."

For many years those words ran through my mind in a too-familiar refrain. Constant repetition made them meaningless, until they had no more significance than the sound of train wheels on a long journey. They were merely part of the everyday accumulation of trifles which, seen too often, seed themselves in the lower stratum of the mind without disturbing its surface and then, moved by some unaccountable force, suddenly germinate at a most unexpected time. That is why one sometimes remembers, quite suddenly and for no reason, the exact shape of a crack in one's nursery ceiling, a broken tile in the floor of a passage at school, or the pattern of a wallpaper in a long-forgotten house.

The whole business of remembering is most intricate and hard to understand. What happens to forgotten sights and experiences and do we ever really forget, or are they all put aside, suitably edited and filed by that tidy and most respectable organ, the mind, like the dusty files of *Punches* behind the curtains in the lobby at Kensington Gore, in the hope that they may be of some use at a future date? Otherwise how can it be that, though for years I could not remember what happened round the corner of a passage in my grandfather's old house on Sydenham Hill, not long ago, during a dream, I turned that corner and there it all was, just as I had last seen it twenty years ago?

I said just now that the mind was respectable. Hypocritical would be a better word, at least for the memory, and I suppose that is part of the mind. Memories are notoriously untrustworthy, not so much in what they forget but in what, after all, should be their chief function—the things they remember. Many honest, unimpeachable men have gone to their graves clearly remembering something which never happened. Take, for example, the pleasing case of the very old man who remembered actually seeing Napoleon. Scholars and historians fastened upon him like leeches. Here was an unrepeatable opportunity to discover some new fact, some hitherto unrecorded personal idiosyncrasy that might throw an entirely new light on the whole of his character. The tone of his voice, his movements, anything that had the touch of actuality. But all the old chap could remember was that the Emperor seemed to be a fine upstanding man with a long white beard. No doubt he saw Napoleon all right, and not somebody else, but he, alone among men, encumbered with his ridiculous memories, knew nothing about his appearance

at all. All of which is a long way from the notice in
my grandfather's downstairs cloakroom.

For years, then, those few simple words ran
through my head unheeded and uncriticized, as
familiar as the tune of the National Anthem:

> "PLEASE HOLD DOWN UNTIL CISTERN
> BE EMPTY."

I must have read it more than three hundred and
sixty-five times in a year without thinking about it.
(One day a more delicate pen than mine may write
a whole volume of reminiscence about these small
but important apartments which play such an un-
chronicled part in our lives. Casting one's mind
back, what a wealth of variety they represent, each
with its own peculiarities. And the essential feature,
the plumbing—what a reflection of the artistic and
cultural tastes of the various periods it shows! "A
Hundred Years of Plumbing"—an irresistible title.
And the keen student would have a reflective feast in
those glazed names alone. The whole history of the
last century of our race might be written round them,
starting with "The Grosvenor", in Old English Gothic
lettering and concluding with "The Civic" in plain
Roman with no serifs.)

For a large part of my childhood I had been dimly
aware of that card, yellowing and faded with the

afternoon sunlight which, in summertime, fell across it. Then one day, owing to one of those minor and unrecorded upheavals of the mind that mark one's growth just as surely as the pencillings on the edge of the nursery door, I read the words with a new, a seeing and a critical eye.

"PLEASE HOLD DOWN UNTIL CISTERN
BE EMPTY"

Why not, I thought for the first time in all those years:

"PLEASE HOLD DOWN UNTIL CISTERN
IS EMPTY"

Was it more correct to say "be empty" than "is empty"? If so, I realized with horror that I had been wrong all my life. I had gone about the world unknowingly making this mistake, which must have been obvious to everyone but myself. It was like those humiliating mispronunciations of adolescence—"Penelowp" for Penelope, "negotate" for negotiate—or the childish nightmare of being left, the only one in church kneeling, when everybody else has stood up. My whole previous life was shown up in a new light. I saw myself walking through the world in ignorance saying "is empty" when everybody behind my back was smiling and excusing my gauche mistake.

That was my first reaction. Then came doubt of

my grandfather himself. Up to now I had looked upon him with the uncritical eye of childhood as being infallible. (What a great deal of trouble would be saved in the world if we could only convince children that we are generally wrong and that most of the information we give them is inaccurate. It is impossible not to teach children. Every time we open our mouths in their presence we teach them something, whether we like it or not, and a good 90 per cent of what we teach them is bigoted, biased and misleading, or else purely misinformed. It is a solemn thought. Even now, owing to some quite unconsidered remark made in front of me when I was a child, I measure a hundred yards in my mind's eye by the distance from the front gate of the house we were living in at the time to the pillar box at the end of the road, and a mile from our house to the railway station. I know quite well they are wrong, but it is too late now. I cannot unlearn what I learned as a child.) "Perhaps," I thought, "it is he who is wrong after all." And with the first crack of doubt the whole precarious structure of confidence collapsed.

No doubt there comes a time when we are ripe for disillusionment and this syntactical problem was rather an instrument than a cause of any change of outlook. It did not occur to me that perhaps my grandfather himself, writing the notice at his study desk years before, may have been troubled with the same doubts about his correctness, or that he might have scribbled "is" on the blotting paper and glanced at it sideways to see what it looked like. Still less did it occur to me that both "is" and "be" might be right; that in nine cases out of ten there is no unassailable right and wrong, no utter black or blank white.

No, either I or my grandfather was wrong. And with my grandfather I began to identify the whole adult world, all that I had accepted so unquestioningly hitherto. The last remnants of a comfortable reliance on face values went and I began to look about for further signs of this conspiracy to deceive and impose upon the credulity of the young.

A casual glance when my mind happened to be in a particularly critical mood had opened the flood gates of doubt. There the little card still remained, yellow and curling with its rusty drawing pin at the top, unchallenged except by myself. I alone in a condoning and hypocritical world.

"PLEASE HOLD DOWN UNTIL CISTERN BE EMPTY"

My eyes were open to the world, to its deceptions and its fallibilities at last.

CHAPTER ELEVEN

THE SWAN OF BAYSWATER

SOMETIMES in the evening, when my grandfather had been to the Petty Sessions, where he sat as a magistrate, he would bring home with him a certain Mr. Whatley, who was, I think, Clerk to the Court. At least, I know that he was a gentleman of some standing in the legal world and that he has since become, not plain "Mr. Whatley", but "Sir Wilfred".

There would be a slight stir in the household when this tall, white-headed figure with its distinguished profile was seen getting out of the car after my grandfather. Aunt Maria would have to move her Patience from the study table to the little conservatory behind the drawing-room and Aunt Pem would also be banished upstairs in case her anxiety to please should cause her fresh paroxysms of laughter.

They made a well-contrasted pair as they walked up the few yards of tiled path from the wrought-iron gate to the front door: Mr. Whatley tall, grave and white, with a swan-like poise and consciousness of his own appearance, and my grandfather, short, red and smiling, trotting beside him on his stiff little legs. As Jonzen opened the front door, letting the roar of traffic swirl like a flood through the downstairs rooms, Aunt Pem, laughing nervously, would be scarcely round the bend of the staircase leading to the drawing-room, and the study, when my grandfather led the way into it, rubbing his hands and clicking his false teeth, would still have that slightly guilty and secretive air of a room too hurriedly and too recently evacuated. My grandfather, aware of this, would rub his hands all the harder and smile more deprecatingly in an endeavour to offset it, and Mr. Whatley would raise his voice with a conscious display of good breeding and carry the conversation himself for a few minutes to put my grandfather at his ease and show that he, as a man of good family and some social standing, knew perfectly how to glide over these uneasy moments and that my grandfather, who had made his money in trade, could not be expected to handle the situation with such suavity and poise.

Occasionally, if Mr. Whatley's approach was more than usually sudden and unheralded, I would find myself trapped in the dark recess of the study with no chance of escape and, after my grandfather had drawn Mr. Whatley's attention to me and he had acknowledged it with a grave and stately inclination of the head, it was more prudent to remain where I was, bowed over the War numbers of *Punch* or Leech's illustrations to *Mr. Sponge's Sporting Tour* in the half darkness of the inner room than to venture past the two seated figures to the hall door. I would sit there turning over the dusty pages, politely pretending to be absorbed, while my grandfather and Mr. Whatley discussed the day's proceedings in Court over a whiskey and soda poured generously by my grandfather and received graciously but not humbly; or while Mr. Whatley recounted a personal anecdote introducing the name of some notoriety whom my grandfather could not be expected to have met. Pouring over *Mr. Sponge* at the dark end of the room I would try not to overhear all that was said, but, with my attention half distracted to my book, the recurrent words "we Whatleys" forced themselves on my mind as they flashed by with the rhythmic insistence of telegraph poles on a train journey.

In recounting these stories about his family, Mr. Whatley was indulging his little weakness in a way that would not have been possible in the presence of one of his own social standing, and it was the price he asked for the honour of his presence in my grandfather's house. All this was understood and tacitly agreed upon as my grandfather sat listening attentively, with a genial smile on his face, or laughed outright, patting himself on the thigh with a stubby hand and said: "Capital, capital!" with the over-appreciative manner of a young schoolboy applauding an older boy and a respected ringleader of his set. My grandfather realized fully that he could not expect the patronage of one of "we Whatleys" without some sacrifice either of dignity or sincerity, so he smiled a little more deprecatingly, laughed with a little more flattery than he actually felt. Like all self-made men whose wealth has come from commerce, my grandfather had a secret contempt for the more favoured professional classes, though he did not show it in their presence. Many, possibly including Mr. Whatley himself, came under the general heading, to quote my grandfather's own words, of those who "couldn't make a living at an apple stall". But this was an opinion only expressed at breakfast, or on some other occasion when my grandfather was alone with his family. Whatever his secret opinion of Mr. Whatley might have been, he hid it under a smiling and respectful exterior and Mr. Whatley, for his part, though he might, with that glazed and uninformative eye, have been noting the mediocrity of our pictures—a photogravure of the child Handel discovered by his parents playing the spinet in a loft and another called "His First Commission", showing a small child drawing a beautiful lady in the dress of Charles the Second, while her cavalier sweetheart looks on—did not for a moment relax his gentlemanly, even friendly manner. For, besides being an excellent listener and one on whom he could safely inflict his little weakness, my grandfather was many times richer than he, though, of course, it was the process of amassing that fortune and the source from which it came that formed the unbridgable gulf between them. On the whole, then, the balance was finely adjusted and each contrived, with a delicate nicety, to keep it so.

However long they chose to sit on, my grandfather with his short legs stretched out on to his hassock and Mr. Whatley with his fine, swan-like profile turned towards me, talking, smiling, nodding their acquiescence—Mr. Whatley to my grandfather's wealth, my grandfather to Mr. Whatley's breeding and position—it would not be possible or correct to disturb them. As dinnertime drew near Jonzen would bustle in and out of the study on the most flimsy pretext, breathing ponderously and hoping, by the frequency of her interruptions, to dislodge them. At last Mr. Whatley would rise and say that he was keeping us from our dinner, and my grandfather, with many polite protestations, would see him to the front door. There would be a sudden gush of sound again as the traffic noise washed and swirled round the passages, a few words of parting on the doorstep— my grandfather warmly and affably inviting Mr. Whatley to call in again another evening and Mr. Whatley assuring him with impeccable politeness that nothing would please him more—then the heavy front door would bang to and once more I would have that feeling of security, of remoteness from the cold, unfriendly world of rushing taxis and limousines, of pale and unassailable Mr. Whatleys.

As soon as the door was closed the house would revert to its old genial simplicity. Jonzen would announce: "Dinner is sairved", Aunt Pem and Aunt Maria would return from the drawing-room and my grandmother would appear from nowhere in particular, for she had a talent for disappearing apparently from the face of the earth when somebody came whom she did not like, and she did not like Mr. Whatley.

The house returned to its old simplicity, but it was

not quite the same, at any rate to me, for Mr. Whatley seemed to linger behind like a chill breath from the outer world. For the first time I noticed that the furniture was extremely old-fashioned and rather tasteless, that Jonzen, as she breathed heavily in the background behind the dining table, should have been a butler. Mr. Whatley seemed to leave behind him a sneer as impalpable but unmistakable as the Cheshire Cat's grin.

The sneer would hang on the air of the dining-room all through dinner. My grandfather, realizing that Mr. Whatley was not popular in the household, became half shamefaced and half resentful, while my grandmother made it as plain as possible that she did not approve of his friend by apologizing to everyone that the dinner was over-cooked and sending a message to Ellen by Jonzen to say that she fully realized that it was not in the least her fault. Aunt Pem, dimly conscious that something was wrong but quite unable to guess what it might be, would try to put my grandfather in a good temper by saying, just as we all felt the subject could not be mentioned any more, that she thought Mr. Whatley a very handsome man and that he really seemed to enjoy coming as he always stayed such a long time.

My own feeling was that, though I was slightly sorry for my grandfather, I also felt he had betrayed us all in some way; that his too subservient manner had allowed the vaguely disquieting sneer to hang behind, like cigar smoke, round the curtains, the pictures and in the upholstery of the chairs. It had been a shock to see him off his guard, so overawed. Before it had always been he who was grand and awe-inspiring. We, as members of his family, had allowed ourselves willingly to be dominated by him. If he said there were to be oysters on Wednesdays there were oysters; if, when somebody was threatened by a wasp, he announced in the solemn tones of a judge pronouncing sentence: "Death seldom ensues", then we were subdued. Now he had sold us all merely for the momentary goodwill of a well-bred but super-cilious swan.

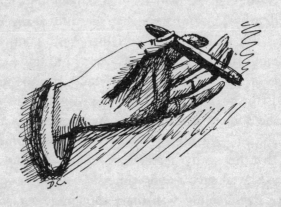

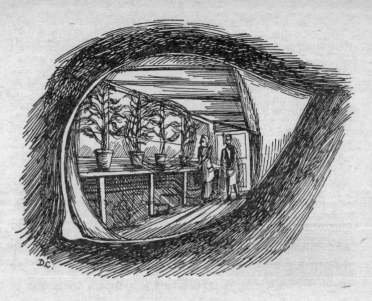

CHAPTER TWELVE

THE DOG'S-EYE VIEW

SOMETIMES it seems that only the tremendous is worth writing about, that everything one reads or writes should be full of mighty catastrophes or upheavals and that nothing less is worth while. Earthquakes, wars, tragedies, and triumphs have stretched our compass to such an extent that the sheer ordinariness of ordinary people and their lives seems absurdly trivial by comparison. But there is a virtue in triviality. I remember looking into a dog's eye when I was a child and being surprised to see reflected, not only myself, but the whole garden. There it all was, complete and exact, in brilliant miniature.

To the truly discriminating human being, if there ever is one, the slightest, most unconsidered action— the striking of a match or a sudden laugh—can be as significant as all the discoveries of science during a lifetime. There it is, the whole world of wars and rumours of wars, of slumps, booms, art and religion, big business and small minds, all reflected, like the garden in the dog's eye, by some unnoticed triviality. The difficult but pleasant task of the hypothetical discerning human being is to observe and decode these trivialities, to translate the banal into terms of the eternal.

Therefore, as my grandfather strutted stiffly across to the farthest corner of the room to pour out his whiskey and soda, I should, with my dog's eye, have been able to reconstruct from it the whole intricate business of civilization. For civilization is organized self-discipline and civilization as a whole, I feel, could not be better expressed than by the figure of my grandfather, anxious for a drink but determined, for his own good, to make it as difficult for himself as possible, stumping across the room whistling "O Rest in the Lord" under his breath and then, when his self-imposed difficulties were overcome, pouring himself out an extra large one.

The real adventures and experiences, then, are small and often unnoticed. In fact, the greatest adventures of all are those of the mind, that happen within ourselves, and the real adventurers are those who can wring experience even from waiting on a railway station, while others may travel round the world or jump out of aeroplanes daily and remain just the same. The Chinese, those masters of harnessing the ordinary, make minature gardens with dwarf trees, as perfect and as satisfying to the cultured eye as an estate, and all in a space no larger than a tea tray.

Carrying this theory to its full extent one might argue that it should not be necessary to travel when one can "see the world in a handful of dust". Didn't I see and experience years ago, as I followed my grandmother round the long greenhouses at Sydenham Hill, the whole of the tropics in miniature, condensed to the size of a glasshouse? (And, after all, what is mere size? Would Botticelli's "Birth of Venus" be any better for being fifty times as big, or Bach's St. Matthew's Passion a hundred times as long?) Now, whenever I smell geraniums, especially in conjunction with blistered hot-water pipes, I am back once more on a Saturday morning following my grandmother down the long perspective of the greenhouse with Ray, the gardener. I am poking idly at the plants, picking the paint blisters in the humid, over-scented atmosphere. Supposing then, after all the trouble and expense of a journey to the tropics, I should find myself, like Alice and the Red Queen, back where I started so long ago on Sydenham Hill?

It is much the same in the sphere of mental adventure and experience. If my grandfather did not actually commit murder there was murder in his eye as it followed a wasp round the breakfast table and into the marmalade pot and then, as he leant slowly towards it, "The Times Newspaper" in one hand and a knife in the other, before squashing, crunching and annihilating it over the table cloth with all the strength in his body. It was a dog's eye tragedy—for the wasp—and, for the time being, my grandfather was a murderer in miniature.

Life at Kensington was placid and uneventful. It went by in a series of days smoothly alike with no melodrama greater than the killing of a wasp, the sudden slamming of a door or, perhaps, somebody whistling in the street at night, but it was none the less life.

CHAPTER THIRTEEN

UPSTAIRS, DOWNSTAIRS

IN the morning, when my grandfather was due to leave for the office, there was always a sharp encounter between Lucy and Jonzen for the honour of putting on his coat. Sometimes Ellen also would take part. Five minutes before the appointed time the hall would be completely empty, with my grandfather's gloves and bowler hat waiting on the table. As soon as he approached, with *The Times* in one hand and his slip-on glasses in the other, humming to himself and trying to look unconscious of the impending scene,

Lucy and Jonzen somehow were there, waiting for him. (They seemed to have the same miraculous powers of manifestation as the ticket collectors in Kensington Gardens. One only has to sit down in an apparently deserted part to find a collector at one's elbow immediately. Many times I have tried to discover how this trick was done and sat deliberately, trying to look in all directions at once, only to hear behind me that deprecating cough and the preparatory ting of the ticket punch. I am forced to the conclusion that, through working for so long on Peter Pan's home ground, they have learned the secret of invisibility. Either that or else the London County Council allows them to live in hollow trees.) Every day the same scene took place. One or other of them would seize his overcoat while the remaining one hovered round, not daring actually to interfere, but determined to make things as difficult as possible for the victor. Between them my grandfather would be pushed this way and that, brushed, patted, shaken and, if Jonzen happened to be successful, pulled right up on tiptoe as he put his arms into his overcoat, for she was a powerful woman, a good head taller than my grandfather, and in the excitement of the moment she frequently forgot her strength.

My grandfather's attitude throughout the whole affair was passive. It was never his habit to question anybody about their job and the daily battle, though it made him feel slightly awkward as the two women fussed about him, tugged down his coat and picking imaginary pieces of fluff from his collar, was all due entirely to excessive zeal. He did not interfere in household questions beyond examining the trades-men's books at the end of the week and glancing over the list of expenses in connection with the car which Parsons always prepared, and I do not remember that he ever questioned anything, for when he did trust anyone—and he trusted everyone whose hair was not red—he did so blindly.

Lucy had been in my grandfather's household forty years and Ellen the same. There was no life to Lucy other than that of my grandfather's family and de-scendants, except for "me sisters"—"me sister Rose", "me sister Alice", "me sister Cassie", "me sister Sarah" and "me sister Lottie". Perhaps in a few generations' time the whole relationship of servant and employer will seem fantastic and absurd. It may be hard to convince anyone that human beings can live together in the same house for years without really knowing one another and without ever saying exactly what they mean. But to our generation the whole careful relationship of deceit and artificiality, of partial kind-ness and generosity on the one side and of partial devotion on the other seems so natural as to be almost unnoticed. It seemed quite normal to us that as soon as the door was closed behind them—or even before—we should repeat stories of their amusing mis-pronunciations ("Good enough for *Punch*, my dear!"), while we knew quite well that downstairs they were laughing at us and probably entertaining their friends at our expense. There is a pleasing element of mutual hypocrisy which, I fancy, will be a rich source of research for future sociologists.

In the elaborate hierarchy of the kitchen and ser-vants' quarters Lucy stood high, as she had been with my grandfather so long. It was really right, then, that she should have helped him on with his coat in the mornings, but then the front door was Jonzen's job, being parlourmaid. So a delicate situation was created which my grandfather, looking rather shamefaced in the midst of this too feminine display of devotion, did not attempt to solve. When he had gone and the front door had slammed to, Lucy would hobble back upstairs to her sewing-room, her face contorted with anxiety—for what nobody could imagine.

It seems that worry and anxiety are necessary constituents of the human mind. If there is nothing reasonable to worry about a cause must be invented. How much more sensible and rational are animals with their so-called lower intelligence. One never sees a dog or cat racked with worry or an anxious expression on the face of a cow. They know quite well that somebody else has the unenviable job of feeding them. Their subsistence is assured, so why should they worry?

Lucy's position was just as secure, yet she was forced to create imaginary dangers to balance her mental dietary. Years before, when my grandfather's family were children, she made them fold their clothes neatly every night by saying: "Supposing the the house was to catch fire, you wouldn't want the firemen to see your clothes put away all any'ow." No domestic animal, relieved of the necessity to struggle for its livelihood, could have achieved such a high degree of imaginative anxiety.

Writing letters was to Lucy what a sewing machine is to a canary. As soon as she saw my mother writing at the study desk she would hover in the background, pick up the copper ash tray with the profile of Mr. Winkle in the bottom, polish it on her apron and put it down again automatically, without knowing what she was doing, then she would say: "Well, ma dear, I don't want to worry you, but . . ." and the unquenchable flow would begin. Perhaps it would be whether or not to light the drawing-room fire or which of the "young girls" was to have a half day, or perhaps about Jonzen, who had a habit of "slipping into a little crépe de chine and going out to get some fresh air in her lungs" at unspecified moments, or perhaps the deeper and more far-reaching problem of spring cleaning. "Well, ma dear, I told yer puppa, I said: 'If I was you,' I said, 'I should only 'ave the front rooms done this year because if you ask me the 'ole of the back of the 'ouse is going to fall out.' But there, it doesn't do to look on the gloomy side, does it? Well, as you know, I always was one to see the funny side meself. Many's the time I've said to old Ellen: 'Well, Ellen,' I've said, 'I wish someone'd give me a good 'it down the spine to make me laugh.'" And she would pause a moment to straighten the ornaments on the mantelpiece—tiny brass figures of Sam Weller and Sairy Gamp which, no doubt, caused Mr. Whatley an inward smile. "But there, it isn't for me to say which rooms 'e 'as done, of course. It's just as 'e says, but . . ." flicking abstractedly with a duster. "Of course I don't want you to think I mind the work. It's not that at all. Well, no one can't say that I was ever one for getting out of the work. Old Ellen, she was always one for a lark. 'Come on, Luce, you're only young once,' she used to say, but I was never so 'appy as when I 'ad somethink to polish. Well, I always did say that the 'appiest 'oliday I ever spent was that time yer mother took the little 'ouse at Woolacombe and I 'ad Master Reggie, Miss Marjory and Miss Winnie down with scarlet fever. Oh, Master

Reggie, 'e was a little terror. The things 'e used to get up to—well there. I couldn't 'elp but laugh, 'e was that comical. Yer mother always used to say: 'Well, Lucy, you 'ave got patience,' but then I was never one to mind what the children did, as you know. Of course, it's not like that now, with these 'young girls'. Not that little Ivy isn't quite a good little thing in some ways, but it isn't like it was with the 'young girls' as I always told yer mother. I told her it's not as though you can say: 'You do sech a thing and I'll put up the curtains' like, if you see what I mean. I 'ope you don't think I'm grumbling, ma dear, because, as you know, I never was one to grumble. I don't even mind doing the grates and that, though I never 'ave been used to doing the fires. As you know, I never was one to mind what I do, but it's just that come the winter it's the dark mornings."

And as my mother retreated up the stairs to the drawing-room she would hear Lucy's voice trailing on to nobody in the study, rising occasionally to shrill vehemence, then lapsing back to a steady reminiscent drone. It did not really matter to her that nobody was listening. Like a true artist she did not depend on an audience. It was art for art's sake. Long after my mother was settled at the desk by the drawing-room window she could hear, far away below, Lucy still talking to no one in an empty room.

The whole relationship of employer and employee was delicate and strange; an elaborate compound of condescension on the one hand and servility on the other. In former days a vast, anonymous army of piano tuners, french polishers and clock-winders crept noiselessly and subserviently in and out of the houses of the well-to-do, moving with the practised silence of a lifetime spent in making themselves as nearly invisible as the too solid flesh of humanity would allow. How many times in our youth have we not heard those odd, unrhythmic notes coming from an apparently deserted drawing-room—an unearthly, mournful noise like the tapping of a lost spirit, as perhaps it was—and been told not to go in because the piano tuner was there? But apart from a strange bowler hat on the hall chair—a bowler hat at once so meek and respectable that it seemed to be saying 'Excuse me, sir' every time one looked at it—and perhaps a grey wraith flitting noiselessly to the front door, there was no actual manifestation of the piano tuner himself. One did not know his name, his religion, politics, or even his size in boots.

This semi-abolition of the physical presence had its drawbacks. When my mother and her sisters were children it was a recognized fact that as soon as the conversation had taken a more than usually ridiculous turn there would be a slight rustling, a gentle cough and the clock man would be among them, shrinking himself into the smallest possible space and trying his hardest to look as though he did not possess the sense of sound, sight or speech. No doubt they felt genuinely sorry for him and may even have said: "Good morning", but it must have been sad to go through life knowing that, as one entered a room, laughter would be smothered and that, before the door was closed behind one, it would burst out again twice as loudly.

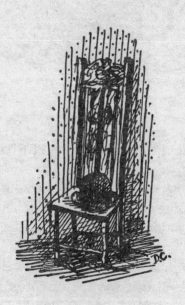

CHAPTER FOURTEEN

THE PLEASURES OF PREJUDICE

MY grandfather, as I have said, was an exceptionally easy-going man. I seldom heard him utter a word of condemnation and never remember having seen him really angry. The worst that his children ever had to fear from him was that he would call one of them a "little goose", that was the extent of his awfulness, and this happened so seldom that, when it did, the effect was all the more powerful.

He had, however, some very fine prejudices apart from red-haired men and boots with toe-caps. One of the best of these was against long telephone conversations. If one of us spoke for more than a few minutes he would lower his *Times* and say with unshakable authority: "The telephone was not made for private conversation," as though he had it from the lips of Mr. Edison himself.

Perhaps this was due partly to the fact that he took to the telephone late in life. He would only use it reluctantly and when he did he would speak with that insulting loudness and clarity that English travellers of the past used when addressing foreigners and, to the last, he opened all telephone conversations with the archaic formula: "Are you there?"

There were many human frailties which my grandfather could pass over with scarcely a frown. In most respects he was exceptionally liberal and humane in his point of view. Drunkenness he accepted, as all lovers of Mr. Pickwick necessarily must, as inevitable —at least in others. He would merely quote an old veterinary friend of his youth who advised him: "Never get drunk before breakfast, Mr. Richard," and leave it at that. All the conventional forms of domestic immorality were so far removed from him that he never even bothered to pass judgment on them. In short, he was the last person to be carping and censorious, but toe-caps or a telephone conversation that was not brutally curt and concise were more than he could bear. All his rational tolerance would disappear at once. "The telephone was not made for private conversation." He spoke with extreme authority because he spoke from prejudice and not from reason.

There is a primitive pleasure in abandoning one's intelligence and giving way to a good prejudice that is like lying back in a bath that one knows to be too hot. From my earliest youth I disliked all children called Ernest. There has never been the slightest reason for this. I was never, to my knowledge, slighted in the cradle by an Ernest. No, my dislike is founded on something far deeper and more lasting than mere reason. (Ernest! There is something furtive, something pale and malignant about the sound of the word.) The amount of harmless pleasure I've had from disliking the name Ernest is incalculable. I only hope that I may never meet an Ernest who disproves my prejudice, or an unlimited joy will be denied me.

I have also derived considerable quiet satisfaction from disliking rhododendrons, pine trees and all the other products of a sandy soil. There may be parts of Surrey and Hampshire—large stretches in the direction of the New Forest—which are both sandy and beautiful, but nothing would induce me to admit it.

Strongly entrenched in my prejudice, impregnably fortified by stupidity, I will not see beauty where there is sand. In a universe shattered with doubts, full of faiths that I would give much to believe in with all my heart, I am completely certain of only two things: that the name Ernest is evil and that there can be no beauty on a sandy soil.

I am certain of these things because I am prejudiced, therefore ignorant about them. For certainty comes only from ignorance, not knowledge, and the most self-confident men are the most stupid. Their confidence is merely a prejudice in their own favour. It comes from that most priceless asset which a benign Providence can bestow—an inability to see any other side to an argument but one's own. Without this inestimable quality no man can rise to greatness in this world. Where there is division or doubt in the mind there is weakness and where there is weakness there can be no authority. Men of authority, I maintain, all have this one quality in common—a great, a shining and an imperishable stupidity. That is, men who truly believe in their authority, who do not know in secret that they are wrong most of the time and who do not wield their authority for its own sake but because they know it to be a necessity, and with the tongue at least partly in the cheek.

Authority itself is irrational. Dr. Johnson's Latin

master beat him for not being able to answer the most abstruse questions. As Johnson said, if he had been able to answer them he would never have gone to school, but all the same he was the first to admit that he owed most of his exceptional knowledge of the classics to this tyrannical man.

Only the luxuriously bigoted, wallowing in the bath of prejudice and turning on the hot tap, really believe that black is black and white is white, he is wrong and I am right. They must be happily ignorant of nine-tenths of the world and—still greater blessing —totally ignorant of themselves. "Where ignorance is bliss", etc. etc. Turn on the hot tap. Let the steam swirl. Lie back and close the eyes. Blessed are the bigoted, for they shall have peace of mind.

CHAPTER FIFTEEN

A PUFF OF CIGAR SMOKE

HISTORY, both personal and universal, could be admirably recorded in smells, if there were any way of perpetuating them. (What a pleasant and instructive record it would be, and what a chance for that neglected, unappreciated organ, the nose!) All that could be said about my grandfather in the space of twenty books could be summed up instantly in one whiff of cigar smoke. It is like the entry of the Demon King in pantomime: a puff of smoke, and out of it comes, not horns and a tail, for nothing could be less demoniacal than my grandfather, especially after dinner, but a round smiling figure with the childlike look of an Edward Lear drawing.

There is a period flavour in cigar smoke reminiscent of distant days of sybaritic ease—like mental waistcoat buttons bursting—that belies my grandfather, for he never smoked more than two cigars a day. He was rigid about this, just as he was rigid about getting up at half-past seven in the morning, having a cold bath— with or without a purple bath mat—and riding with his friends in the Row. Though he enjoyed making money—and there is no doubt that he did immensely enjoy it for its own sake—he also took great pleasure in living far below his income. Indulgence, to him, was even more exquisite when it was curbed and disciplined. That is why he made himself walk from one end of the room to the other for his nightly whiskey. To have had it beside him would have been cheating. It would have been short-circuiting the law on which his whole life had been founded: the law of overcoming obstacles. He knew that the whole secret of value is in rarity, so he rarely allowed himself pleasures and when he did they were all the more pleasant.

Cigar smoke and the sound of horses' hoofs, how unfailingly they evoke the sight of my grandfather

returning from the office in a phaeton driven by old
Bob Smith! Already my grandfather, who one felt
would certainly live for ever, a symbol of immortality,
seems to have sunk into the improbable past. Then
one whiff of cigar smoke—something happens inside
the nose, messages are sent hurriedly to the brain.
There is a consultation. Mental archives are searched,
files are examined under the letter H for "hands
(gouty)" and C for "countenance (red)". My grandfather always used the word "countenance" instead of
"face". All women, or nearly all, he would admit to
be beautiful, pretty or, at the least, pleasing, but the
most he would say of any man was that he had a "nice
open countenance". Then, in the space of a hundredth
part of a second or so I am back in the house in
Kensington Gore with the study fire leaping and the
curtains drawn. My grandfather is squinting down his
nose, in his arm-chair by the smoking table, to see
whether his cigar is properly alight; there are two
new books from Mudie's library on the table with
the evening paper; Jonzen has just gone out of the
door into her pantry breathing heavily and, in some
odd way, I feel, disapprovingly as though she had a
grievance; and we are in for another evening of the
indecipherable *Fortunes of Nigel*.

With the smell still in my nose I can remember
what I had forgotten for many years; that, though

they were happy evenings and I had nothing but respect and affection for my grandfather, Nigel and his fortunes brought a feeling of frustration, almost of claustrophobia. The evening paper was there on the table. I could see it out of the corner of my eye. I longed to emerge from Nigel's world of dusty verbosity into the comparative reality of journalism. It would have been like coming out of a long tunnel into sudden daylight. And it was not only Nigel. That smell of cigar smoke also reminds me that, happy though it was, it was a period of suppression and insincerity. There were many tastes and opinions to be suppressed and held, passionately, in secret. For, though I rebelled against Nigel and all he stood for in art, literature, music and politics, I had not the moral courage to say so openly in the face of overwhelming opposition, and continued to express admiration where I did not feel it and pretended to views which I had long since ceased to hold. At the age of seventeen I felt myself to be leading a double life. There I sat, after a good dinner, in front of the study fire about to read, with apparent pleasure, the novels of Scott, whom I detested and, in my lofty adolescence, despised heartily, while all the time I was a secret radical, heretic and unbeliever. Because my opinions were held in secret they were all the more dear to me. I was like an early Christian in a heathen land,

I felt, as I sat pretending to enjoy Scott and Dickens by my grandfather's fireside, burning—ungratefully, as it now seems—with a fierce, disruptive light within.

Jonzen comes in with another scuttle-full of coal, breathing more heavily and more disapprovingly than ever. It is going to be a warm, cosy evening in the study at Kensington. My grandfather draws hard at his cigar once or twice. Then takes it out to see how it is burning. Satisfied that it is well alight he sits back and expands into a smile. There is a short pause while he abandons himself to the first ambrosial puffs. The fire leaps and dances. Traffic in the street, somewhere beyond the heavy curtains of the study window, rumbles by with steady, deadened roar which accentuates the feeling of well-fed security inside my grandfather's study. Outside in London it is theatre time. Lighted buses hurry along Kensington Gore towards the West End, each a cosmos in itself. Taxis whisk the furred and bejewelled from the immunity of their own doorsteps into the stream. The dim-lit pavements are full of disembodied footsteps. In the half light every girl seems unbelievably beautiful. Typists who, in the cruel reality of morning, are plain and unnoticeable, are now, as they trip along by the Park railings or wait in dark clusters at the bus stops, all as promising of perfection as the veiled beauties of the East. Theatreland is brilliant. The taxis which swooped to the pavement in Pont Street, Queen's Gate and Prince's Gardens, unload their gorgeous passengers and slide away into oblivion. Pit queues are beginning to shuffle forward hopefully while the street entertainers rush through the last part of their performance with one eye on the street corner. Everywhere there is bustling chaos and an undercurrent of Rabelaisian vitality. The population of London has changed completely; the whole tempo has accelerated. The door of a saloon bar opens and a man comes out, shouts something back over his shoulder, there is a roar of laughter and a glimpse of a smoking, beer-smelling crush. The door slams to. The man stops, spits and goes off still grinning at his own cleverness. It is quiet in the Park. Hunched figures stand pressed together in the darkness while the passer-by tries hard to pretend that they do not exist. It looks a miserable business, this speechless love-making in dark archways and park benches. The passer-by hurries on apologetically to his family and fireside with a feeling partly of sympathy and partly of self-righteousness. He hurries on into the little pool of lamplight, then on into darkness once more, past the next seat with its single figure, dark and still in the half light. White legs and a white face, shadowed eye sockets that might be looking at one or might not.

My grandfather blows out a long breath and the smoke coils and eddies up towards the inverted electric light bowl in the centre of the room, where a frenzied fly is buzzing madly to and fro trying to get out. "Well, my boy," my grandfather says at last, "where did we leave our friend Nigel last night? He'd just met old Sir Mungo Malagrowther, if I remember rightly." The buses outside stop at the pavement opposite, pick up their loads and groan on. The evening paper lies on top of the library books unread. I go over to the heavy old bookcase and draw *The Fortunes of Nigel* from its place in the standard edition of the Waverley Novels and my grandfather, beaming all over his kindly face, settles himself down for the evening.

DENIS CONSTANDUROS

CHAPTER SIXTEEN

A REARGUARD ACTION

A LL through my childhood the possibility that my
grandfather would not live for ever did not enter
my head. It was not to be contemplated that there
could be an existence without either the house on
Sydenham Hill or the one at Kensington Gore. It was
impossible also to imagine a life without, somewhere
in the background, that solid and reassuring mass of
wealth and prestige, never publicly mentioned but as
essential to the conditioning of our private universe
as the law of gravity itself.

After all, he behaved as though he intended to live for ever, in spite of his breakfast-time recital of obituaries and fatal accidents which seemed to bring him such comfort. Those daily habits, the temperate restrictions on smoking or drinking by daytime; all carefully planned and rigidly executed, set in motion a rhythmical process which my grandfather himself would have been powerless to stop. Indeed, it sometimes seemed as though these habits became too much for him, as though they bore him along at a pace livelier than that of his own choosing, like a man on a bicycle with no brakes when he comes unexpectedly to a steep hill. He was in a dilemma. Jealous of his reputation as a Remarkable Old Man, he continued with his hunting and his awe-inspiring ablutions, but in doing so he ran the risk of killing himself and thus spoiling his record.

For many years, indulging his preference for all kinds of frugality, he went to his office by bus. He would leave the house at the same moment every morning and plunge, one felt, spiritually naked, into the rapids of London's work-going traffic—or if not naked, then clothed only in a sense of self-preservation tuned to hansom cabs and horse-drawn buses. After many perilous moments in which my grandfather, slightly bewildered and clutching his bowler hat to his head, seemed to be buffeted hither and thither like a cork in the lethal stream, he would reach the bus stop on the other side and, boarding a number 46 or 52, not only would he climb to the top out of bravado, but make his way down the lurching aisle to the very front seat. There, as he was borne away out of sight towards Knightsbridge, we could see him settle down with a look of satisfaction on his face, waiting for the supreme moment when the conductor came to collect his fare—for he had a free pass.

Then, as he approached his eightieth year, the brakeless bicycle he had made for himself began to gather speed and my grandfather, still committed to his spartan way of living, came gradually to realize in his heart that the pace was too much for him. The realization came, I think, very slowly and he fought it back hour by hour, knowing that once the careful routine was broken he would be abandoned to old age. (That is the disadvantage of a carefully-planned, abstemious and hard-working life. In the end the abstemious worker is in the same predicament as the habitual drunkard. Deny one his bottle and the other his office desk or his cold bath and each is reduced to ruin. The inference is obvious. Work, when in-dulged to excess, is just as much of a vice in the eyes of an all-seeing Nature as dipsomania.) He became pathetically glad of an excuse not to have his cold bath, he was troubled by mysterious stiffness in arms and legs and a persistent cough. Though he struggled tenaciously he was forced to give ground week by week, month by month, with the certain knowledge that each inch yielded could never be regained.

He began going to doctors. One very distinguished specialist, a riding acquaintance, whom he consulted about his cough, merely told him that at his age he was lucky to be able to cough at all—and charged him five guineas. He went through all the stages of self-delusion and hope, of secret and unexpressed disappointments, of new cures that were to succeed where all else had failed but which, after a day or two, were tactfully not mentioned again. Still he continued to grow more and more lame. Then, with the pioneering spirit which persuaded him to open the marmalade pot after so many years, he tried osteopathy. Whether it was the stimulus of trying something new I do not know, but at any rate a battle was won in his perpetual rearguard action against old age, a valuable amount of time gained. He resumed his early morning rides, his old Pickwickian *joie de vivre*, and even, when no adequate excuse could be found to relieve him, the detestable cold bath. Wednesday evenings saw him once more in the blue-spotted waistcoat, with a dozen oysters before him and a glass of sherry wine at his side. Summer evenings were once again spent trotting round the solemn, sunlit galleries of Burlington House with his marked catalogue open in his hand and the slip-on glasses ready if he should want to peer closely at a particular piece of brushwork or a signature; or else dozed away in the no less solemn precincts of the Oval, in the shadow of those venerated gasometers, watching Hobbs make one of his quiet, gentlemanly centuries.

It was a brief Indian Summer and I think he knew it as he sat on the hard benches of the Members' Stand or paused on one of the hot gratings in Burlington House to admire once more a particular favourite. The inevitable conclusion could not be long delayed, so he made the most of each day and crowded as much happy, unsensational living as he could into it. Before very long, he knew, his own obituary notice would be read out, to mingle with the crunching of toast at many other breakfast tables.

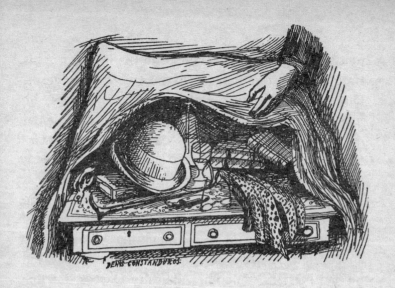

CHAPTER SEVENTEEN

DERBY DAY 1928

IN the beginning of his seventy-eighth year my grandfather went for a cruise in the Mediterranean where he picked up a germ and developed a bad fever. As soon as he arrived home he went to bed. But he was obviously very ill and within a week or ten days he was dead. At the time Lucy blamed herself entirely for not packing his thicker pants, as though, deterred by the extra wool, the germ might have turned back.

It was always rather a grief to me that a man so deeply and essentially English, so representative of

131

much, both good and less good, in the England of his time, should have fallen a victim to a foreign germ. One felt that, with his almost naive insularity, he must have been as defenceless against continental diseases as he was baffled by continental pronunciation. One felt also that he was well fortified to resist all upright, above-board English ailments, such as gout or high blood pressure, but that this was a mean and treacherous attack from an unexpected quarter.

Apart from this there was much that was strangely appropriate in his death, for it was Derby Day and he had been to something like fifty Derbys, rattling through south London and over Epsom Downs in the coach-and-four which belonged to the business. Also it was seven-thirty in the morning, the exact moment when the little knot of friends was collecting round the mounting block in the Gardens opposite. It was a fine morning in early summer—and Derby Day. (It was also, rather unfortunately for my grandfather, the fourth of June, so that those members of the medical profession who were not at Epsom were at Eton.) If my grandfather was killed by a foreign germ he chose to die on the most typically English day in all the year. My grandmother might have said that it was selfish of him to die just when he knew that everybody wanted to go to the Derby, but I think it was a last gesture of defiance—it was the same spirit of petulance that caused him, on the mornings when he had written her the household cheque, to leave my grandmother at the front door without turning round or even raising his hat. Perhaps it was also the same streak of hardness as that which caused him to read out, every Christmas, on the morning of the day when he had promised to take his family to the pantomime: "We are very sorry to state that Aladdin has been taken ill and will not be able to appear this afternoon," and then to watch the look of dismay and disappointment cross the faces of his children.

The junk in the boxroom has been sifted through; all the dust sheets thrown back and their muddled, inconsequent treasures examined. My grandfather at the window acknowledging the salute of the passing coach with a flourish of his cigar—a glitter of bright paint, a flash and clatter of brass in the afternoon sunlight and the vision is gone with a rhythm of hoofs and a rumble of wheels that carry it away round the curve in time, towards Kensington Palace and eternity, and leaves Aunt Pem, a disembodied smile, still following it with her eyes from the long drawing-room window.

Pull back another sheet and there is my grandfather setting out across Kensington Gardens in the gathering gloom, drawn by the invisible force which compelled him, as soon as he knew it was closing time, to cross the Gardens alone, like a rowing boat on the Atlantic, while the handbells tolled, keepers' voices wailed like spirits through the trees and lights in neighbouring buildings or buses outside the railings snapped on one by one.

Or perhaps it is Sunday afternoon and we are expecting some of his riding friends to tea. The drawing-room fire is alight, though it is really not needed. The drawing-room fire is Jonzen's job and her heavy breathing, as she brings in the silver teapot and cake stand, shows, in the telepathic manner of servants, that she did not intend to have to lay it again this season. We stand at the drawing-room windows in our best clothes, watching the top of Queen's Gate if it is to be Mr. Meadows, the good natured, jovial banking friend who, like my grandfather, still wears the top hat and morning coat of a vanished era. Or if it is to be the two Miss Andersons from Bayswater, who tell such delightfully amusing stories without a smile, but with hats that nod knowingly when the point is reached, then we shall be looking in the other direction, down the gardens towards the Albert Memorial, where a few decorous promenaders are examining the first crocuses, pausing a moment in the sun.

Under another sheet are the carved wood smoking table and the old blue-spotted waistcoat, mute reminders of my grandfather at ease, of Jorrocks, Pickwick, and My Uncle Toby, of winter nights with the curtains drawn, of "The Times Newspaper" and "sherry wine". They are somehow romantic, and at the same time a trifle pathetic now, like the stage properties of some long-disbanded theatrical company —shabby, but still with a faint whiff of faded glamour about them.

Lot four, ladies and gentlemen: one grey bowler hat, worn by my grandfather at the Van Horse Parade, held at the Royal Botanical Gardens, Regent's Park and, occasionally, when my grandmother insisted that he should go, to the gardens of Chelsea Hospital for the Flower Show. Also one catalogue of the Summer Exhibition of the Royal Academy, for the year 1927, heavily marked at all pleasantly seductive landscapes, with a preference for racehorses or roses, or at all portraits of particularly beautiful and virtuous-looking women—and a membership ticket for the Oval, much thumbed, of the same date.

The dust sheets are all back in place once more, the remnants of my grandfather, a little decayed here and faded there, a little frayed by forgetfulness and nibbled by time, are reinterred. The heavy front door has closed for the last time, shutting out the rumbling traffic and the superciliousness of the swan-like Mr. Whatley, Jonzen has heaved her last gusty sigh of complaint and the last cold bath has gurgled down the waste-pipe into the bowels of the earth, the last soda-water syphon has spluttered abruptly into silence.

My mother goes across the room on that morning of Derby Day 1928. It is fine and sunny, with an air of gentle beginning that promises good things to come. In the Royal College of Music, by the Albert Hall, the usual morning cacophony of voices, violins and pianos has started, and out in the street already the traffic has that look of holiday about it, as though everything, even buses and taxis themselves, is going to Epsom Downs for the day. Down below, just inside Kensington Gardens, the little group of friends has gathered round the mounting block, waiting for the horses. They look up at the house and talk among themselves, as though uncertain whether to send someone over to inquire. Then, as my mother pulls down the blinds (generally used by Lucy to keep the sun off the new mahogany bedsteads), they realize that it is too late and turn away. Everyone in the house is suddenly hushed, except Lucy, who, downstairs in an empty room, audibly laments that she did not think of those thick pants.